SNAPPY SAYINGS

Wit & wisdom from the world's greatest minds

Bradford G. Wheler

BookCollaborative.com

Cazenovia, New York

SNAPPY SAYINGS

By Bradford G. Wheler

Wit & wisdom from the world's greatest minds

Second Edition Copyright 2014 by Bradford G. Wheler

First Edition Copyright 2009
All rights reserved. This book may not be reproduced, transmitted, or stored in whole or in any part by any means, including graphic, electronic, or mechanical without the express consent of the publisher except in the case of brief quotations embodied in critical articles and reviews.

BookCollaborative.com
P.O. Box 403
Cazenovia, NY 13035
Editor@www.BookCollaborative.com

ISBN-13 978-0-9822538-7-8

Humor & Wit, Quotations, History & Criticism

Cover and Interior Design by AuthorSupport.com

Printed in the United States of America

Also by Bradford G. Wheler

GOLF SAYINGS: wit & wisdom of a good walk spoiled

CAT SAYINGS: wit & wisdom from the whiskered ones

HORSE SAYINGS: wit & wisdom straight from the horse's mouth

DOG SAYINGS: wit & wisdom from man's best friend

EIGHTEEN 6/10/71: The Poetry of John G. Hunter III

SNAPPY SAYINGS: wit & wisdom from the world's greatest minds

INCA'S DEATH CAVE: An Archaeological Mystery Thriller

(Coming in 2015)

LOVE SAYINGS: wit & wisdom of romance, courtship, and marriage

Contents

Acknowledgments v
Foreword by Jay Walker vii
Introduction ix

Chapter 1: Money 1
Chapter 2: Advice 15
Chapter 3: Work 27
Chapter 4: The Professions 39
Chapter 5: The Arts 53
Chapter 6: Education 65
Chapter 7: Sports 77
Chapter 8: Drink 89
Chapter 9: Sex 103
Chapter 10: Love 117
Chapter 11: Marriage 129
Chapter 12: Women 143
Chapter 13: Man 157
Chapter 14: Children 171
Chapter 15: Human Nature 185
Chapter 16: Truth & Lies 199
Chapter 17: Politicians 213
Chapter 18: Democracy 225
Chapter 19: Religion 237
Chapter 20: Death 251
Chapter 21: Youth & Aging 263
Chapter 22: Life & Happiness 277

Appendix Biographies 291
Index of Quotations by Author 409

ACKNOWLEDGMENTS

This book is the result of years of love and enjoyment of history, art, humor, and the English language. I'm not sure how to thank all the people in my life who helped with this process. My parents and relatives for sure, many fine teachers and professors, also my interesting and engaging friends, I need to thank them all.

A few people deserve special thanks for their direct involvement in this book. My wife Julie for encouraging me to do something with the thousands of quotations I collected and had collecting dust in the closet. My niece Anne Redmond for not only encouraging me to produce this book but agreeing to give up much of her January break from Cornell to work on the book with me. Without her artist's eye and computer skills I never would have gotten off dead center. She made the work fun and helped form the vision of what I hope is a somewhat insightful but mostly fun book.

Also a very special thank you to my dear friend Jay Walker for his thoughtful foreword. Jay is a true lover of books and has one of the finest private libraries in the country. I've known Jay since the mid 1970s when we lived together as members of the Sigma Phi Society at Cornell University. His genius, audacity, and energy are only exceeded by his generous giving of himself to his family and friends.

I owe a great deal to several professionals without whom I could never have completed the book. Nancy Kelner who took my hand-written quotations and my cut-and-paste biographies and turned them into working documents. Michelle and Jerry Dorris at AuthorSupport.com for interior and cover design and layout. I also want to thank them for all the hand holding they did. There were so many things I didn't know about producing a book. Simom, Ethan, and their co-workers on the one-to-one training team at the Apple Store for patiently working on my computer skills. Thank you to my web designer Brian Hoke at Bentley & Hoke LLC. Your work is just beginning. I also want to thank the support staff at Lightning Source Inc.

Thank you all for not only helping me with this book but opening my eyes to several new and fun projects.

Foreword

Pithy quotations, much like jokes, play an unusual role in our lives. Though we are hard pressed to remember more than a few of them, their impact runs much deeper. As they are consumed, they seem to bypass our memory pathways and go directly to some special place in the brain that allows us to feel the words, like a kind of music. The sentences, like notes, disappear, and an emotion is called forth as if reading were not involved. This is the "magic" of a written communication that reaches us at a very different level.

Much as we do not have to think about laughing, to instantly laugh at a humorous anecdote or saying, the same is true to feel the essential truth of a quotation — a few short words that we intuitively recognize as revealing an insight, a confirmation, or a connection to our rich patterns of experience.

A collected book of quotations presents us with an unusual challenge. It is not a book to be read in the classic sense of a sequential story. Though it can be used as reference book for speechwriters, that is not the intent with this volume. There are far larger and more weighty volumes filled with every imaginable quote. And, of course, the Internet opens a world of a billion saying and quotations to endlessly browse.

Instead, the author has taken the hard task of culling and selecting from a world of infinite possibilities and combinations, much like a master distiller must carefully select and blend his ingredients to offer up a sensation both pleasant and stimulating. His goal is simple. If successful, we might sit back and simply enjoy the sensation of a thought that has stood the test of time.

The result is a book to be tasted or sipped, much like one might pour oneself a small after-dinner drink from a bar stocked with hundreds of exotic liqueurs. Drink too much or mix them together, and the effect is lost. Select and savor just the right one, and a meal becomes a memory.

As you open a page at random and choose your elixir, you are transported to another place and time. Whether it is the smile of irony, the nod of recognition, or the slight shake of the head that reminds us, "oh, how true that is," the joy of a wonderful quotation is not in the remembering or repeating of it, but in the simple act of allowing it to melt into the fabric of the mind, like some cotton candy of thought, sweet, ephemeral, and yet deeply satisfying in a wonderful and human way.

Jay Walker

Mr. Walker is the founder of Priceline.com and Walker Digital. He is the recipient of Cornell University's 2009 Entrepreneur of the Year Award.

INTRODUCTION

This book didn't start as a book. It certainly didn't start as a part of a new business publishing venture (BookCollaborative.com) that marries the Internet, outsourcing, social networks, and on demand printing. My original idea was to collect fun "snappy" quotations you could enjoy reading and maybe actually use in a speech, or toast, or at a party. I envisioned an indexable card system. The cards would fit in your pocket for quick reference and re-file themselves for future retrieval by topic. It was a variation on the old library card file system, for those of us old enough to remember that.

Thus started my decades long collection of hand-written 3-by-5 inch index cards of "Snappy Sayings". As the number approached 3,000 and the topic-indexed file boxes became yards long, I realized I was facing a time when I would actually have to do something with these wonderful words.

I decided to perfect my indexable, auto-re-filing, pocket-fitting card system. Thus Joke Box/Quote Box was, if not born, at least conceived. I determined the practical size of the cards to fit in your pocket. How many easy to read lines per card. How many cards per Joke Box/Quote Box. How many index topics per box, and on and on. On paper, I had it figured out. Of course manufacturing, distributing, and marketing an unknown product that looked sort of like a book and by 2000 was outperformed by the simplest of computer databases was somewhat problematic.

Deciding to leave these practical problems for later, I plowed ahead based on my calculations. Eighteen topics per Joke Box/Quote Box, about twelve cards per topic and about three "Snappy Sayings" per card. Now I had the parameters to produce the content for the first Joke Box/Quote Box. Just pick the best 700 – 800 quotations out of my 3,000 index cards of "Snappy Sayings", organize them into 18 topics of about 12 sheets in a way that would be really fun, no… GREAT FUN to read and use.

I poured over my index card collection, selecting about 1600 – 1700 "Snappy Sayings" organizing them into twenty-two groups. Then I reduced it to 800 or so organized in page order for the twenty-two topics. I carefully placed each page group of index cards on the face of the photocopier and I had my hand-written draft of "Snappy Sayings".

That's where the project stalled for about five years. In December 2007, my wife asked if I was ever going to do anything with that book stuff in the cabinet? It's not really a book. It's, well, it's sort of hard to explain. Her comment was "maybe it should be a book".

Around Christmas I was visiting with my niece Anne who was home from Cornell. Somehow the topic came up. Anne said, "Why not do a book, you can always do your box thing later." That, along with her offer of help, persuaded me to knock the five years of dust off my draft and produce this book.

During this period I was reading several interesting books

(*Wikinomics, Groundswell, The Innovator's Solution, Microtrends, Predictably Irrational, Seeing What's Next, Strategic Intuition, Outliers, Buy-ology*, and others) and thinking there had to be better business models than my last business. As the book progressed the idea for a business venture took shape. The book became a vehicle to develop a collaborative publishing venture using twenty-first century technical devel-opments and focusing on two areas of personal enjoyment, Wit & Wisdom and Art & Artists. For a detailed explanation go to www.BookCollaborative.com.

With BookCollaborative.com's first publication what you get is about 800 "Snappy Sayings" illustrated and organized into twenty-two chapters. These "Snappy Sayings" are distilled from many thousands of quotations I have read. They have been filtered through my unique and _____ (you fill in the blank) worldview and sense of humor.

My hope is you will find it funny, insightful and enjoyable. Really what I want is for you to have GREAT FUN with "Snappy Sayings" from some of the brightest and wittiest minds of all times. It is also my hope that the second edition of *Snappy Sayings* will replace most of the current illustrations with original art and photos from collaborating artists. As you read through the book, if any of your drawings, photos, or paintings better fits the spirit of the quotations on that page go to www.BookCollaborative.com and suggest that they be included in the second edition of *Snappy Sayings*.

       Bradford G. Wheler
       Cazenovia, N.Y. 2009

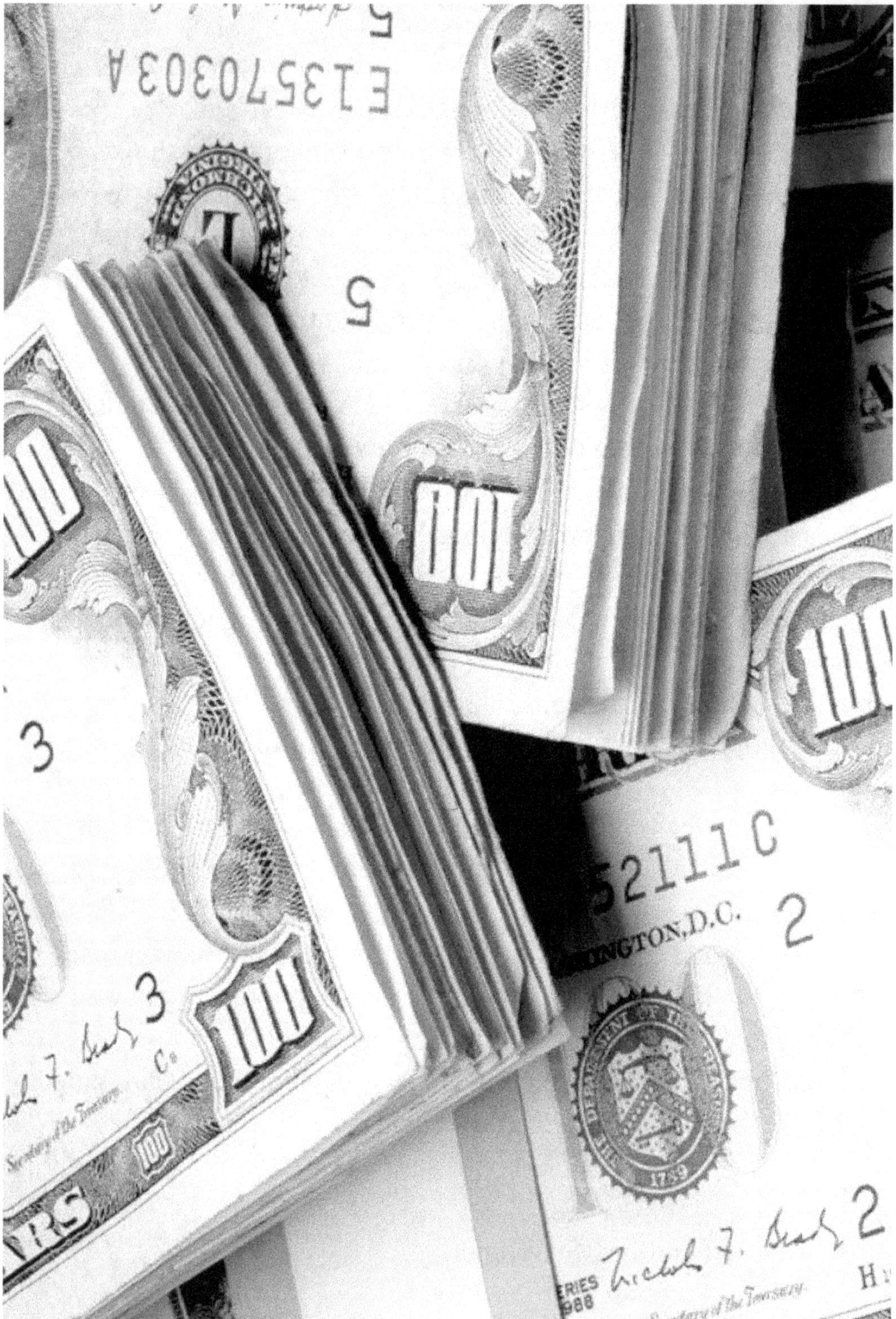
52111C
Secretary of the Treasury

CHAPTER 1

Money

Honesty is the best policy – when there is money in it.

- MARK TWAIN (1835 – 1910)

Creditors have better memories than debtors.

- BENJAMIN FRANKLIN (1706 – 1790)

I'm a rich man as long as I don't pay my creditors.

- TITUS MACCIUS PLAUTUS (255 – 184 BC)

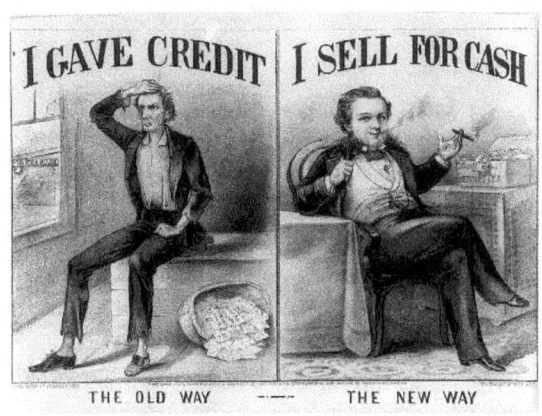

Nothing is so well fortified that money cannot capture it.

- CICERO (106 – 43 BC)

In this world nothing is certain but death and taxes.

- BENJAMIN FRANKLIN (1706 – 1790)

Money-getters are the benefactors of our race, to them …. are we indebted for our institutions of learning, and of art, our academies, colleges and churches.

- P. T. BARNUM (1810 – 1891)

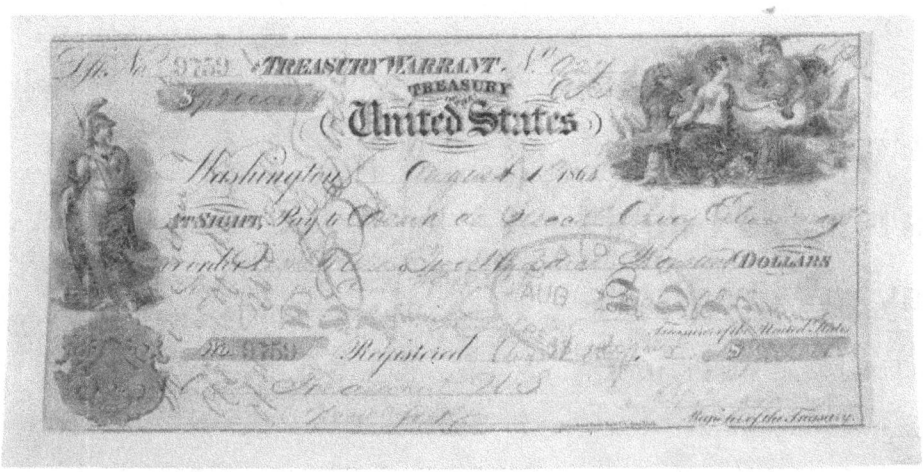

Canceled Check From the Alaska Purchase

I've been rich and I've been poor – and believe me, rich is better.

- Sophie Tucker (1884 – 1966)

By the time we've made it, we've had it.

- Malcolm Forbes (1919 – 1990)

The two most beautiful words in the English language are "check enclosed".

- Dorothy Parker (1893 – 1967)

I enjoy being a highly overpaid actor.

- ROGER MOORE (1927 –)

Cocaine is God's way of telling you you've got too much money.

- ROBIN WILLIAMS (1951 –)

I hope you'll accept my personal IOU. It's worth its weight in gold.

- W. C. FIELDS (1880 – 1946)

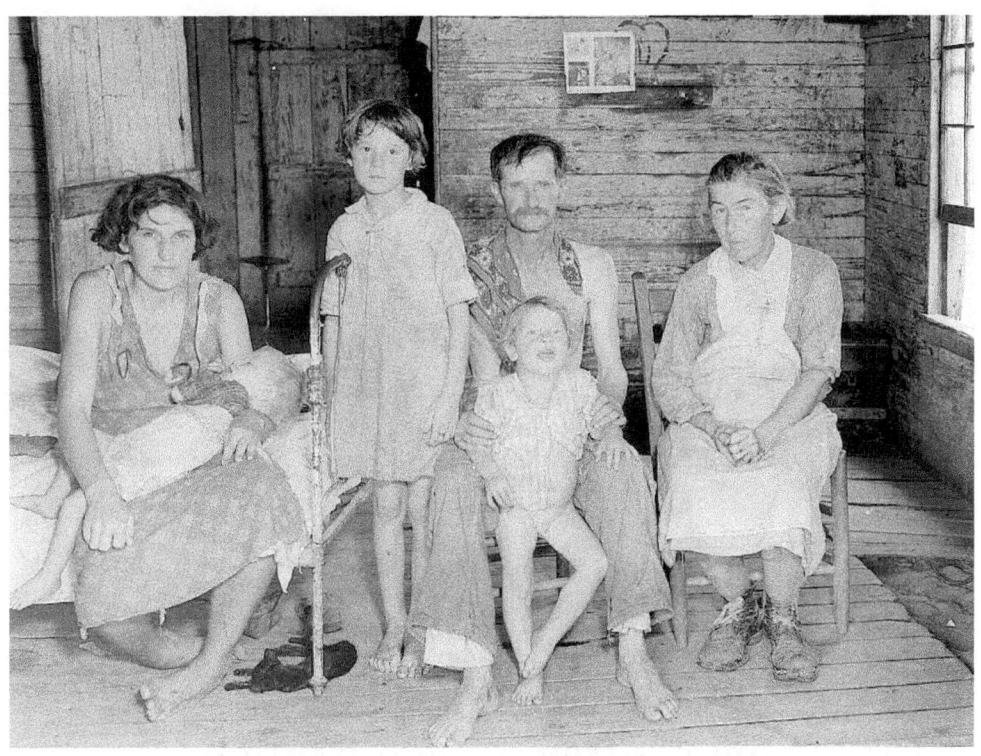

I believe that the power to make money is a gift from God.

- JOHN D. ROCKEFELLER (1839 – 1937)

Lack of money is the root of all evil.

- GEORGE BERNARD SHAW (1856 – 1950)

I'd like to live like a poor man with lots of money.

- PABLO PICASSO (1881 – 1973)

Money often costs too much.

- RALPH WALDO EMERSON (1803 – 1882)

**After a certain point, money is meaningless.
It ceases to be the goal.
The game is what counts.**

- ARISTOTLE ONASSIS (1906 – 1975)

**Money is better than poverty,
if only for financial reasons.**

- WOODY ALLEN (1935 –)

The trouble with being poor is that it takes up all of your time.

- Willem De Kooning (1904 – 1997)

Gentility is what is left over from rich ancestors after the money is gone.

- John Ciardi (1916 – 1986)

Virtue has never been as respectable as money.

- Mark Twain (1835 – 1910)

**While you're saving your face,
you're losing your ass.**

- Lyndon B. Johnson (1908 – 1973)

**A billion here, a billion there – pretty soon
it adds up to real money.**

- Senator Everett Dirksen (1896 – 1969)

**A nickel ain't worth
a dime anymore.**

- Yogi Berra (1925 –)

When it is a question of money, everybody is of the same religion.

- Voltaire (1694 – 1778)

It is only by not paying one's bills that one can hope to live in the memory of the commercial classes.

- Oscar Wilde (1854 – 1900)

Saving is a very fine thing. Especially when your parents have done it for you.

- Winston Churchill (1874 – 1965)

Make money and the whole nation will conspire to call you a gentleman.

- George Bernard Shaw (1856 – 1950)

The chief value of money lies in the fact that one lives in a world in which it is overestimated.

- H. L. Mencken (1880 – 1956)

Money doesn't satisfy greed; it stimulates it.

- Publilius Syrus (85 – 43 BC)

They say that money talks, but the only thing it ever said to me was goodbye.

- JOE LOUIS (1914 – 1981)

Nobody works as hard for his money as the man who marries it.

- FRANK MCKINNEY "KIN" HUBBARD
(1868 – 1930)

My problem lies in reconciling my gross habits with my net income.

- ERROL FLYNN (1909 – 1959)

Income-tax returns are the most imaginative fiction being written today.

- Herman Wouk (1915 –)

The income tax has made more liars out of the American people than golf has.

- Will Rogers (1879 – 1935)

The hardest thing in the world to understand is income tax.

- Albert Einstein (1879 – 1955)

Chapter 2
Advice

Whoever fights a monster should see to it that in the process he does not become a monster.

- Friedrich Wilhelm Nietzsche (1844 – 1900)

No man can think clearly when his fists are clenched.

- George Jean Nathan (1882 – 1958)

He is more likely to contribute heat than light to discussion.

- Woodrow Wilson (1856 – 1924)

It is better to debate a question without settling it than to settle a question without debating it.

- JOSEPH JOUBERT (1754 – 1824)

Plato

Wise men talk because they have something to say, fools because they have to say something.

- PLATO (424/423 – 348/347 BC)

Wisdom comes by disillusionment.

- GEORGE SANTAYANA (1863 – 1952)

To receive a favor is to sell your liberty.

- PUBLILIUS SYRUS (85 – 43 BC)

'Tis an ill cook that cannot lick his own fingers.

- WILLIAM SHAKESPEARE (1564 – 1616)

He that lies down with dogs shall rise up with fleas.

- BENJAMIN FRANKLIN (1706 – 1790)

Every man who will not have softening of the heart must at last have softening of the brain.

- G. K. CHESTERSON (1874 – 1936)

Neville Chamberlain & Adolf Hitler

The one sure way to conciliate a tiger is to allow oneself to be devoured.

- Konrad Adenauer (1876 – 1967)

May God defend me from my friends; I can defend myself from my enemies.

- Voltaire (1694 – 1778)

The word friend is common, the fact is rare.

- Phaedrus (15 BC – 50 AD)

Franklin D. Roosevelt, 1931

When you get to the end of your rope, tie the knot and hang on.

- Franklin D. Roosevelt (1882 – 1945)

Genius is 1 percent inspiration and 99 percent perspiration.

- Thomas Alva Edison (1847 – 1931)

You may have genius. The contrary is, of course, probable.

- Oliver Wendell Holmes (1841 – 1935)

There's always something about your success that displeases even your best friends.

- MARK TWAIN (1835 – 1910)

Even a paranoid can have enemies.

- HENRY KISSINGER (1923 –)

Failure has no friends.

- JOHN F. KENNEDY (1917 – 1963)

A great many people think they are thinking when they are merely rearranging their prejudices.

- WILLIAM JAMES (1842 – 1910)

Minds are like parachutes: They only function when open.

- THOMAS ROBERT DEWAR (1864 – 1930)

Nothing in the world is more dangerous than sincere ignorance and conscientious stupidity.

- MARTIN LUTHER KING, JR. (1929 – 1968)

There is only one good – knowledge; and only one evil – ignorance.

- SOCRATES (470 – 399 BC)

**An idea isn't responsible
for the people who believe in it.**

- Don Marquis (1878 – 1937)

**Greater than the tread of mighty armies
is an idea whose time has come.**

- Victor Hugo (1802 – 1885)

**Consistency requires you to be as ignorant
today as you were a year ago.**

- Bernard Berenson (1865 – 1959)

Character is much easier kept than recovered.

- THOMAS PAINE (1737 – 1809)

Consider yourself a great orator if you can talk yourself into unpleasant duties.

- PUBLILIUS SYRUS (85 – 43 BC)

Thomas Paine

Experience is not what happens to a man. It is what a man does with what happens to him.

- ALDOUS HUXLEY (1894 – 1963)

The measure of a man's real character is what he would do if he knew he would never be found out.

- THOMAS BABINGTON MACAULAY (1800 – 1859)

He can compress the most words into the smallest ideas of any man I have ever met.

- Abraham Lincoln (1809 – 1865)

There is no expedient to which a man will not go to avoid the labor of thinking.

- Thomas Edison (1874 – 1931)

No one ever went broke underestimating the taste of the American public.

- H. L. Mencken (1880 – 1956) / P. T. Barnum / (1810 – 1891)

When a man seeks your advice, he generally wants your praise.

- LORD CHESTERFIELD (1694 – 1773)

He that is good for making excuses is seldom good for anything else.

- BENJAMIN FRANKLIN (1706 – 1790)

There is nothing so absurd but some philosopher has said it.

- CICERO (106 – 43 BC)

Chapter 3

Work

The reason w why worry kills more people than work is that more people worry than work.

- Robert Frost (1878 – 1963)

If you have a job without aggravations, you don't have a job.

- Malcolm Forbes (1919 – 1990)

Work is much more fun than fun.

- Noel Coward (1899 – 1973)

There's no such thing as a free lunch.

- Milton Friedman (1912 – 2006)

Moderation is a fatal thing. Nothing succeeds like excess.

- Oscar Wilde (1854 – 1900)

Take a chance. Remember; Lady Godiva put everything she had on a horse.

- W. C. Fields (1880 – 1946)

Necessity never made a good bargain.

- Benjamin Franklin (1706 – 1790)

There are three kinds of lies: lies, damned lies, and statistics.

- Mark Twain (1835 – 1910)

Every crowd has a silver lining.

- P. T. Barnum (1810 – 1891)

If you make money quickly you must economize quickly or you'll quickly go hungry.

- Titus Maccius Plautus (255 – 184 BC)

Some folks can look so busy doing nothing that they seem indispensable.

- Frank McKinney "Kin" Hubbard (1868 – 1930)

Thunder is good, thunder is impressive; but it is lightning that does the work.

- Mark Twain (1835 – 1910)

Always be smarter than the people who hire you.

- Lena Horne (1917 – 2010)

False becomes true when the boss decides it is.

- Publilius Syrus (85 – 43 BC)

Meetings are indispensable when you don't want to do anything.

- JOHN KENNETH GALBRAITH (1908 – 2006)

A conference is a gathering of important people who singly can do nothing, but together can decide that nothing can be done.

- FRED ALLEN (1894 – 1956)

Meetings are an addictive, highly self-indulgent activity that corporations and other large organizations habitually engage in only because they cannot actually masturbate.

- DAVE BARRY (1947 –)

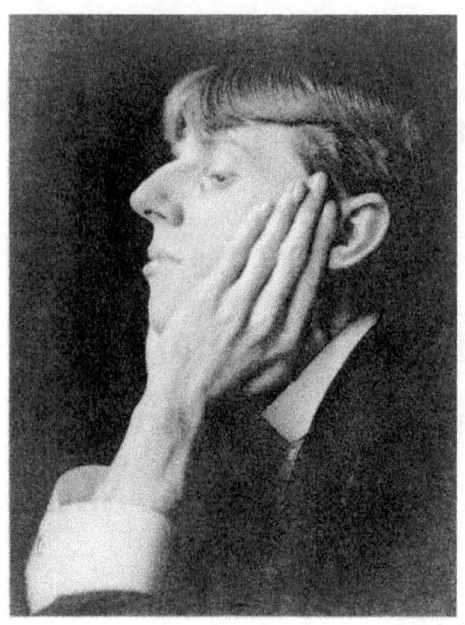

Idealism is fine, but as it approaches reality the costs become prohibitive.

- WILLIAM F. BUCKLEY, JR.
(1925 – 2008)

Idealism increases in direct proportion to one's distance from the problem.

- JOHN GALSWORTHY (1867 – 1933)

The worst form of inequality is to try to make unequal things equal.

- ARISTOTLE (384 – 322 BC)

By working faithfully eight hours a day, you may eventually get to be boss and work twelve hours a day.

- Robert Frost (1878 – 1963)

If ants are so busy, why do they attend so many picnics?

- W. C. Fields (1880 – 1946)

I do not like work even when someone else does it.

- Mark Twain (1835 – 1910)

Housework can kill you if done right.

- Erma Bombeck (1927 – 1996)

My father taught me to work; he did not teach me to love it.

- ABRAHAM LINCOLN (1809 – 1865)

Hard work is damn near as overrated as monogamy.

- HUEY P. LONG (1893 – 1935)

The world is full of willing people; some willing to work, the rest willing to let them.

- ROBERT FROST (1878 – 1963)

The brain is a wonderful organ. It starts working the moment you get up in the morning and does not stop until you get into the office.

- ROBERT FROST (1878 – 1963)

The trouble with the rat race is that even if you win you're still a rat.

- LILY TOMLIN (1939 –)

Work is of two kinds; first altering the position of matter at or near the earth's surface relatively to other matter; second telling other people to do so. The first kind is unpleasant and ill paid – the second is pleasant and highly paid.

- BERTRAND RUSSELL (1872 – 1970)

Charles Lindbergh

Choose a job you love and you will never have to work a day in your life.

- Confucius (551 – 479 BC)

I don't know the key to success, but the key to failure is trying to please everybody.

- Bill Cosby (1937 –)

Luck is a matter of preparation meeting opportunity.

- Oprah Winfrey (1954 –)

I couldn't wait for success so I went ahead without it.

- JONATHAN WINTERS (1925 – 2013)

It takes twenty years to make an overnight success.

- EDDIE CANTOR (1892 – 1964)

When down in the mouth, remember Jonah. He came out all right.

- THOMAS EDISON (1847 – 1931)

Chapter 4

The Professions

Being a hero is about the shortest lived profession on earth.

- Will Rogers (1879 – 1935)

Every profession has its secrets …. If it hadn't, it wouldn't be a profession.

- H. H. Munro "Saki" (1870 – 1916)

The physician can bury his mistakes, but the architect can only advise his client to plant vines.

- Frank Lloyd Wright (1867 – 1959)

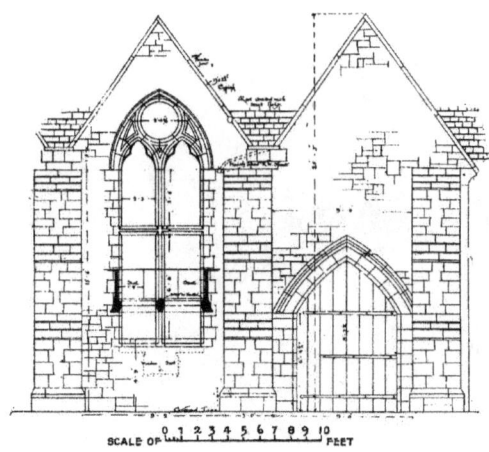

Architecture is frozen music.

- Johann Wolfgang Goethe (1749 – 1832)

If all economists were laid end to end, they would not reach a conclusion.

- George Bernard Shaw (1856 – 1950)

An economist is a man who couldn't tell the difference between chicken salad and chicken shit.

- Lyndon B. Johnson (1908 – 1973)

A doctor's reputation is made by the number of eminent men who die under his care.

- GEORGE BERNARD SHAW (1856 – 1950)

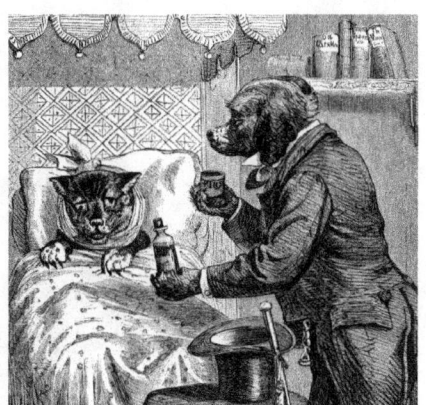

God heals and the doctor takes the fee.

- BENJAMIN FRANKLIN (1706 – 1790)

He had had much experience of physicians, and said "the only way to keep your health is to eat what you don't want, drink what you don't like and do what you'd druther not."

- MARK TWAIN (1835 – 1910)

The best doctors in the world are Doctor Diet, Doctor Quiet and Doctor Merryman.

- Jonathan Swift (1667 – 1745)

It's amazing the little harm they do when one considers the opportunities they have.

- Mark Twain (1835 – 1910)

Doctors and lawyers must go to school for years and years often with little sleep and with great sacrifice to their first wives.

- Roy G. Blount, Jr. (1941 –)

A lawyer with his briefcase can steal more than a thousand men with guns.

- Mario Puzo (1920 – 1999)

Lawyers are the only persons in whom ignorance of the law is not punished.

- Jeremy Bentham (1748 – 1832)

…. as scarce as lawyers in heaven.

- Mark Twain (1835 – 1910)

A successful law suit is the one worn by a policeman.

- ROBERT FROST (1870 – 1963)

Agree, for the law is costly.

- WILLIAM CAMDEN (1551 – 1623)

Lawyers spend a great deal of time shoveling smoke.

- OLIVER WENDELL HOLMES, JR. (1841 – 1935)

Homer has taught all other poets the art of telling lies skillfully.

- Aristotle (384 – 322 BC)

There is no money in poetry; but then there is no poetry in money, either.

- Robert Graves (1895 – 1985)

T. S. Eliot

In the case of many poets, the most important thing for them to do is to write as little as possible.

- T. S. Eliot (1888 – 1965)

> **Free verse is like free love; it is a contradiction in terms.**
>
> - G. K. Chesterton (1874 – 1936)

> **All bad poetry springs from genuine feelings.**
>
> - Oscar Wilde (1854 – 1900)

> **A poet more than thirty years old is simply an overgrown child.**
>
> - H. L. Mencken (1880 – 1956)

William Shakespeare

There are no dull subjects, there are only dull writers.

- H. L. Mencken (1880 – 1956)

After writing for fifteen years, it struck me I had no talent for writing. I couldn't give it up. By that time, I was already famous.

- Mark Twain (1835 – 1910)

Never let a domestic quarrel ruin a day's writing. If you can't start the next day fresh, get rid of your wife.

- Mario Puzo (1920 – 1999)

The covers of this book are too far apart.

- AMBROSE BIERCE (1842 – 1914)

**This is not a novel to be tossed aside lightly.
It should be thrown with great force.**

- DOROTHY PARKER (1893 – 1967)

**A well-written life is almost as rare as a
well-spent one.**

- THOMAS CARLYLE (1795 – 1881)

Without music, life would be a mistake.

- Friedrich Wilhelm Nietzche (1844 – 1900)

Wagner's music is better than it sounds.

- Mark Twain (1835 – 1910)

**I don't know anything about music.
In my line, you don't have to.**

- Elvis Presley (1935 – 1977)

Anything that is too stupid to be spoken is sung.

- Voltaire (1694 – 1778)

Of all noises, I think music is the least disagreeable.

- Samuel Johnson (1709 – 1784)

Only sick music makes money today.

- Friedrich Wilhelm Nietzche (1844 – 1900)

CHAPTER 5
The Arts

There are moments when art attains almost the dignity of manual labor.

- OSCAR WILDE (1854 – 1900)

Art is a jealous mistress.

- RALPH WALDO EMERSON (1803 – 1882)

If you could say it in words, there would be no reason to paint.

- EDWARD HOPPER (1882 – 1967)

**Every time I paint
a portrait,
I lose a friend.**

- JOHN SINGER SARGENT (1856 – 1925)

**A work of art is useless
as a flower is useless.**

- OSCAR WILDE (1854 – 1900)

**Everyone wants to understand painting.
Why don't they try to understand the
singing of the birds? People love the night,
a flower, everything which surrounds them,
without trying to understand them.
But painting – that they must understand.**

- PABLO PICASSO (1881 – 1973)

If that's art, I'm a Hottentot!
- HARRY S. TRUMAN (1884 – 1972)

Modern art is what happens when painters stop looking at girls and persuade themselves that they have a better idea.
- JOHN CIARDI (1916 – 1986)

Abstract art is a product of the untalented, sold by the unprincipled, to the utterly bewildered.
- AL CAPP (1909 – 1979)

Art, like morality, consists of drawing the line somewhere.

- G. K. Chesterton (1874 – 1936)

I'm glad the old masters are all dead and I only wish they had died sooner.

- Mark Twain (1835 – 1910)

The great tragedy of the artistic temperament is that it cannot produce any art.

- G. K. Chesterton (1874 – 1936)

A dramatic critic is a man who leaves no turn unstoned.

- GEORGE BERNARD SHAW (1856 – 1950)

Critics are eunuchs at a gang-bang.

- GEORGE BURNS (1896 – 1996)

A good review from the critics is just another stay of execution.

- DUSTIN HOFFMAN (1937 –)

The play was a great success but the audience was a total failure.

- OSCAR WILDE (1854 – 1900)

There's less in this than meets the eye.

- TALLULAH BANKHEAD (1902 – 1968)

I didn't like the play, but then I saw it under adverse conditions – the curtain was up.

- GEORGE S. KAUFMAN (1889 – 1961)

I don't understand anything about the ballet; all I know is that during the intervals the ballerinas stink like horses.

- Anton Chekhov (1860 – 1904)

I love acting. It is so much more real than life.

- Oscar Wilde (1854 – 1900)

Acting: It is the most minor of gifts and not a very high class way to earn a living. After all, Shirley Temple could do it at the age of four.

- Katharine Hepburn (1907 – 2003)

Actresses will happen in the best regulated families.

- OLIVER HERFORD (1863 – 1935)

Always remember before going on stage, wipe your nose and check your flies.

- SIR ALEC GUINNESS (1914 – 2000)

Modesty in an actor is as fake as passion in a call girl.

- JACKIE GLEASON (1916 – 1987)

An actor's a guy who, if you ain't talking about him ain't listening.

- MARLON BRANDO (1924 – 2004)

A celebrity is a person who works hard all his life to become well known, then wears dark glasses to avoid being recognized.

- Fred Allen (1894 – 1956)

Scratch an actor and you'll find an actress.

- Dorothy Parker (1893 – 1967)

A sign of celebrity is that his name is often worth more than his service.

- Daniel J. Boorstin (1914 – 2004)

A celebrity is one who is known to many persons he is glad he doesn't know.

- H. L. Mencken (1880 – 1956)

You'd be surprised how much it costs to look this cheap.

- Dolly Parton (1946 –)

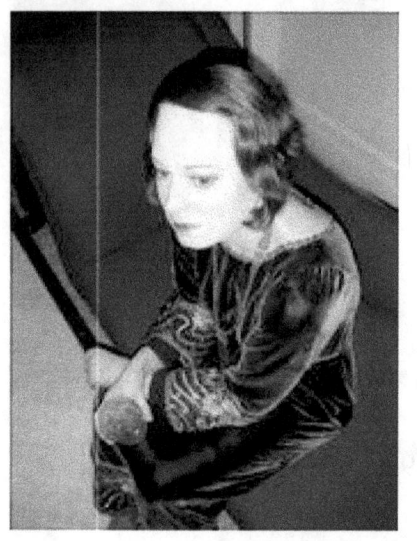

Hollywood is a place where they place you under contract instead of under observation.

- Walter Winchell (1897 – 1972)

Dorothy Parker

The only "ism" Hollywood believes in is plagiarism.

- Dorothy Parker (1893 – 1967)

They didn't release that movie, it escaped.

- Samuel Goldwyn (1882 – 1974)

The Arts

The Hollywood tradition I like best is called "sucking up to the stars".

- JOHNNY CARSON (1925 – 2005)

A producer shouldn't get ulcers; he should give them.

- SAMUEL GOLDWYN (1882 – 1974)

Hollywood is the only place in the world where an amicable divorce means each one gets 50 percent of the publicity.

- LAUREN BACALL (1924 –)

Chapter 6
Education

Education is the best provision for old age.

- Aristotle (384 – 322 BC)

A little learning is a dangerous thing.

- Alexander Pope (1688 – 1744)

The roots of education are bitter, but the fruit is sweet.

- Aristotle (384 – 322 BC)

The school of hard knocks is an accelerated curriculum.

- Menander (342 – 291 BC)

Two things reduce prejudice: education and laughter.

- Laurence J. Peter (1919 – 1990)

Education: That which reveals to the wise, and conceals from the stupid, the vast limits of their knowledge.

- Mark Twain (1835 – 1910)

Soap and education are not as sudden as massacre but they are more deadly in the long run.

- MARK TWAIN (1835 – 1910)

I must say I find television very educational. The minute somebody turns it on, I go to the library and read a good book.

- GROUCHO MARX (1890 – 1977)

I took a speed-reading course and read *War and Peace* in twenty minutes. It involves Russia.

- WOODY ALLEN (1935 –)

It doesn't make much difference what you study, so long as you don't like it.

- FINLEY PETER DUNNE (1867 – 1936)

Education: The path from cocky ignorance to miserable uncertainty.

- MARK TWAIN (1835 – 1910)

Education: The inculcation of the incomprehensible into the indifferent by the incompetent.

- JOHN MAYNARD KEYNES (1883 – 1946)

Is sloppiness in speech caused by ignorance or apathy? I don't know and I don't care.

- WILLIAM SAFIRE (1929 – 2009)

Men are born ignorant, not stupid; they are made stupid by education.

- BERTRAND RUSSELL (1872 – 1970)

A learned blockhead is a greater blockhead than an ignorant one.

- BENJAMIN FRANKLIN (1706 – 1790)

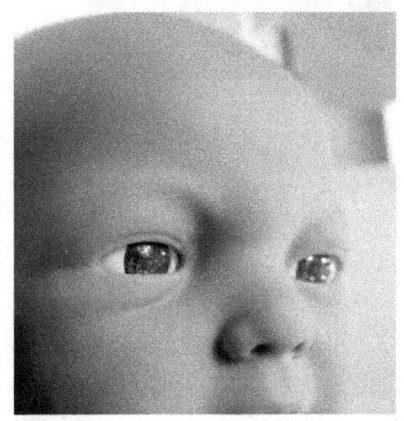

The schools ain't what they used to be and never was.

- WILL ROGERS (1879 – 1935)

I have never let my schooling interfere with my education.

- MARK TWAIN (1835 – 1910)

Lyndon B. Johnson

You ain't learning nothing when you're talking.

- LYNDON B. JOHNSON (1908 – 1973)

Wit is educated insolence.

- ARISTOTLE (384 – 322 BC)

My education was dismal. I went to a series of schools for mentally disturbed teachers.

- WOODY ALLEN (1935 –)

"Whom are you?" said he, for he had been to night school.

- GEORGE ADE (1866 – 1944)

I don't give a damn for a man that can spell a word only one way.

- MARK TWAIN (1835 – 1910)

Education is what you must acquire without any interference from your schooling.

- MARK TWAIN (1835 – 1910)

Transferring gases.

His lack of education is more than compensated for by his keenly developed moral bankruptcy.

- WOODY ALLEN (1935 –)

When you educate a man you educate an individual; when you educate a woman you educate a whole family.

- ROBERT M. MACIVER (1882 – 1970)

A child only educated at school is an uneducated one.

- GEORGE SANTAYANA (1863– 1952)

Education is the ability to listen to almost anything without losing your temper or your self-confidence.

- ROBERT FROST (1878 – 1963)

Those who educate children well are more to be honored than they who produce them; for these only gave them life, those the art of living well.

- Aristotle (384 – 322 BC)

Wonder is what the philosopher endures most; for there is no other beginning of philosophy than this.

- Plato (424/423 – 348/347 BC)

In large states, public education will always be mediocre, for the same reason that in large kitchens the cooking is usually bad.

- Friedrich Wilhelm Nietzche (1844 – 1900)

Those teachers and schools that truly succeed are those which inspire their students to move beyond the expectation of conventional wisdom.

- James D. Watson (1928 –) (co-discovered DNA)

Learning is not child's play; we cannot learn without pain.

- Aristotle (384 – 322 BC)

Old men are always advising young men to save money. That is bad advice. Don't save every nickel. Invest in yourself. I never saved a dollar until I was forty years old.

- Henry Ford (1863 – 1947)

You may have noticed the less I know about a subject the more confidence I have, and the more new light I throw on it.

- Mark Twain (1835 – 1910)

As long as one keeps searching, the answers come.

- Joan Baez (1941 –)

**He who can, does.
He who cannot, teaches.**

- George Bernard Shaw (1856 – 1950)

Chapter 7

Sports

Golf is the most fun you can have without taking your clothes off.

- Chi Chi Rodriguez (1935 –)

The more I practice, the luckier I get.

- Jerry Barber (1916 – 1994)

I never pray to God to make a putt. I pray to God to help me react good if I miss a putt.

- Chi Chi Rodriguez (1935 –)

Golf and sex are about the only things you can enjoy without being good at it.

- Jimmy Demaret (1910 – 1983)

Ninety percent of the putts that fall short don't go in.

- Yogi Berra (1925 –)

He who has the fastest golf cart never has a bad lie.

- Mickey Mantle (1931 – 1995)

When you win, nothing hurts.

- Joe Namath (1943 –)

There are two sorts of losers – the good losers, and the ones who can't act.

- Laurence J. Peter (1919 – 1990)

I hate all sports as rabidly as a person who likes sports hates common sense.

- H. L. Mencken (1880 – 1956)

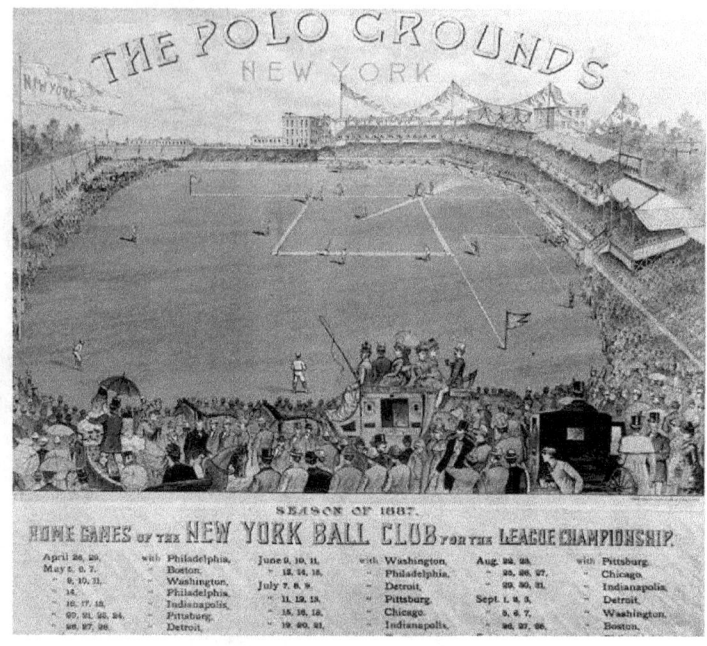

Baseball is ninety percent mental. The other half is physical.

- Yogi Berra (1925 –)

When I was a kid, I wanted to play baseball and join the circus. With the Yankees, I've been able to do both.

- Graig Nettles (1944 –)

I'm not disloyal. I'm the most loyal player money can buy.

- Don Sutton (1945 –)

I knew I was in trouble when they started clocking my fastball with a sundial.

- Joe Magrane (1964 –)

It ain't bragging if you can do it.

- Dizzy Dean (1910 – 1974)

Going to bed with a woman never hurt a ball player. It's staying up all night looking for them that does you in.

- Casey Stengel (1890 – 1975)

**Boxing is like jazz.
The better it is,
the less people
appreciate it.**

- GEORGE FOREMAN (1949 –)

**My toughest fight was
with my first wife.**

- MUHAMMAD ALI (1942 –)

**I know a lot of people
think I'm dumb.
Well, at least I ain't
no educated fool.**

- LEON SPINKS (1953 –)

I'm so fast I could hit you before God gets the news.

- Muhammad Ali (1942 –)

Sometimes Howard [Cosell] makes me wish I was a dog and he was a fireplug.

- Muhammad Ali (1942 –)

Hurting people is my business.

- Sugar Ray Robinson (1921 – 1989)

I went to a fight the other night and a hockey game broke out.

- Rodney Dangerfield (1921 – 2004)

The fans love the fighting. The players don't mind. The coaches like the fights. What's the big deal?

- Don Cherry (1934 –)

He who lives by the cheap shot dies by the cross-check.

- Stan Fischler (1932 –)

We get nose jobs all the time in the NHL, and we don't even have to go to the hospital.

- BRAD PARK (1948 –)

I skate to where the puck is going to be, not where it has been.

- WAYNE GRETZKY (1961 –)

The trouble with officials is they just don't care who wins.

- TOMMY CANTERBURY (?)

The fascination of shooting as a sport depends almost wholly on whether you are at the right or wrong end of the gun.

- P.G. Wodehouse (1881 – 1975)

To brag little – to show well – to crow gently, if in luck – to pay up, to own up, and to shut up, if beaten are the virtues of a sporting man.

- Oliver Wendell Holmes (1841 – 1935)

When man wants to murder a tiger, he calls it sport; when a tiger wants to murder him, he calls it ferocity.

- George Bernard Shaw (1856 – 1950)

There is no use in your walking five miles to fish when you can depend on being just as unsuccessful near home.

- Mark Twain (1835 – 1910)

The race is not always to the swift nor the battle to the strong, but that's the way to bet.

- Damon Runyon (1884 – 1946)

Horse sense is a good judgment which keeps horses from betting on people.

- W. C. Fields (1880 – 1946)

Wherever I go people are waving at me. Maybe if I do a good job, they'll use all their fingers.

- Frank King (1883 – 1969)

When you are not practicing, remember someone is practicing, and when you meet him, he will win.

- Ed Macauley (1928 –)

FRESH AND COLD

DIRECT FROM THE
NORTH POLE.

LITH. BY A. HOEN & CO. BALTIMORE, MD.

PUBLISHED BY F. KLEMM, No. 254 N. CENTRAL AVE., BALTIMORE.

Chapter 8

Drink

Drink is your enemy – love your enemies.

- W. C. Fields (1880 – 1946)

One more drink and I'd be under the host.

- Dorothy Parker (1893 – 1967)

Any one who hates dogs and loves whiskey can't be all bad.

- W. C. Fields (1880 – 1946)

Candy is dandy but liquor is quicker.

- Ogden Nash (1902 – 1971)

Drink, pretty creature, drink.

- William Wordsworth (1770 – 1850)

I'm not so think as you drunk I am.

- Sir John Squire (1884 – 1958)

An alcoholic is someone you don't like who drinks as much as you do.

- DYLAN THOMAS (1914 – 1953)

Hangover: The wrath of grapes.

- DOROTHY PARKER (1893 – 1967)

A woman drove me to drink, and I never even had the courtesy to thank her.

- W. C. FIELDS (1880 – 1946)

Water, taken in moderation, cannot hurt anybody.

- Mark Twain (1835 – 1910)

The best audience is intelligent, well educated, and a little drunk.

- Alben W. Barkley (1877 – 1956)

I drink to make other people more interesting.

- George Jean Nathan (1882 – 1958)

I have taken more out of alcohol than alcohol has taken out of me.

- WINSTON CHURCHILL (1874 – 1965)

Champagne: In victory you deserve it; in defeat you need it.

- NAPOLEON BONAPARTE (1769 – 1821)

Winston Churchill

This wine is forty years old. It certainly doesn't show its age.

- CICERO (106 – 43 BC)

He that drinks fast, pays slow.

- BENJAMIN FRANKLIN (1706 – 1790)

I saw a notice which said "Drink Canada Dry" and I've just started.

- BRENDEN BEHAN (1923 – 1964)

A man must believe in something. I believe I'll have another drink!

- W. C. FIELDS (1880 – 1946)

Abstainer: A weak person who yields to the temptation of denying himself a pleasure.

- Ambrose Bierce (1842 – 1914)

I have to think hard to name an interesting man who does not drink.

- Richard Burton (1925 – 1984)

If you drink, don't drive. Don't even putt.

- Dean Martin (1917 – 1995)

Now don't say you can't swear off drinking, it's easy. I've done it a thousand times.

- W. C. Fields (1880 – 1946)

The secret of drunkenness is that it insulates us in thought, whilst it unites us in feeling.

- Ralph Waldo Emerson (1803 – 1882)

I don't drink water; it rusts pipes.

- W. C. Fields (1880 – 1946)

The Germans are exceedingly fond of Rhine wines. One tells them from the vinegar by the label.

- Mark Twain (1835 – 1910)

I've made a rule never to drink by daylight and never to refuse a drink after dark.

- H. L. Mencken (1880 – 1956)

I like liquor – its taste and effects – and that is just the reason why I never drink it.

- Thomas "Stonewall" Jackson (1824 – 1863)

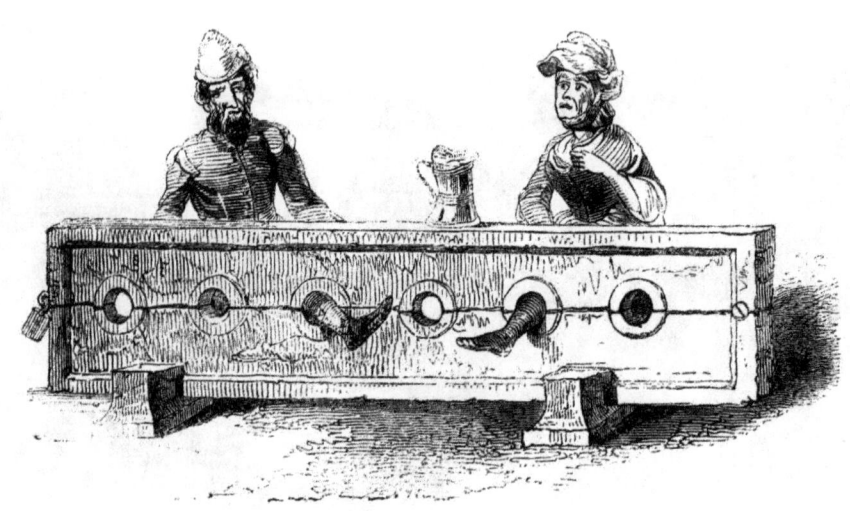

Beer is proof that God loves us and wants us to be happy.

- BENJAMIN FRANKLIN (1706 – 1790)

Drink! For you know not whence you come nor why. Drink! For you know not why you go, nor where.

- OMAR KHAYYAM (1048 – 1131)

Sometimes too much to drink is barely enough.

- MARK TWAIN (1835 – 1910)

Always do sober what you said you'd do drunk. That will teach you to keep your mouth shut.

- Ernest Hemingway (1899 – 1961)

Alcohol is the anesthesia by which we endure the operation of life.

- George Bernard Shaw (1856 – 1950)

He who has not been at a tavern knows not what a paradise is.

- Henry Wadsworth Longfellow (1807 – 1882)

I'm only a beer teetotaler, not a champagne teetotaler. I don't like beer.

- George Bernard Shaw (1856 – 1950)

One of the disadvantages of wine is that it makes a man mistake words for thoughts.

- Samual Johnson (1709 – 1784)

I never said all Democrats are saloonkeepers; what I said was all saloonkeepers are Democrats.

- Horace Greeley (1811 – 1872)

Prohibition officers raiding the Lunch Room of 922 Pa. Ave Wash. D.C. 23792   4/25/23.

Chapter 9

Sex

My brain is my second favorite organ.

- Woody Allen (1935 –)

I can remember when the air was clean and sex was dirty.

- George Burns (1896 – 1996)

Sex alleviates tension, love causes it.

- Woody Allen (1935 –)

If it is worth doing, it is worth doing slowly … very slowly.

- GYPSY ROSE LEE (1911/1914 – 1970)

Sex is good, but not as good as fresh sweet corn.

- GARRISON KEILLOR (1942 –)

You cannot separate young limbs and lechery.

- WILLIAM SHAKESPEARE (1564 – 1616)

Of all the sexual aberrations, the most peculiar is chastity.

- Rémy De Gourmont (1858 – 1915)

If men could get pregnant, abortion would be a sacrament.

- Florynce "Flo" Kennedy (1916 – 2000)

It is one of the superstitions of the human mind to have imagined that virginity could be a virtue.

- Voltaire (1694 – 1778)

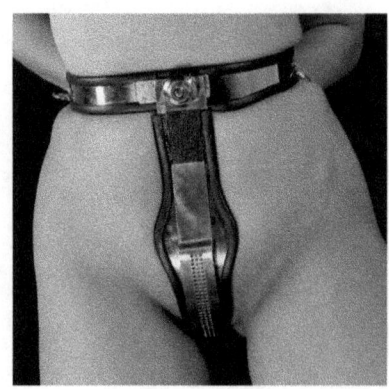

Dear Lord: Give me chastity and self restraint, but not yet.

- Saint Augustine (354 – 430)

You gotta learn that if you don't get it by midnight, chances are you ain't gonna get it; and if you do, it ain't worth it.

- Casey Stengel (1891 – 1975)

Why should we take advice on sex from the pope? If he knows anything about it, he shouldn't.

- George Bernard Shaw (1856 – 1950)

She may be good for nothing, but she's not bad for nothing.

- Mae West (1893 – 1987)

The big difference between sex for money and sex for free is that sex for money usually costs less.

- Brendan Behan (1923 – 1964)

Whoever called it necking was a poor judge of anatomy.

- Groucho Marx (1890 – 1977)

Woody Allen

Bisexuality immediately doubles your chances for a date on Saturday night.

- WOODY ALLEN (1935 –)

If only it was as easy to banish hunger by rubbing the belly as it is to masturbate.

- DIOGENES "THE CYNIC" (412 – 323 BC)

Masturbation! The amazing availability of it.

- JAMES JOYCE (1882 – 1941)

The good thing about masturbation is that you don't have to dress up for it.

- Truman Capote (1924 – 1984)

Hey! Don't knock masturbation. It's sex with someone I love.

- Woody Allen (1935 –)

Celibacy is not hereditary.

- Oscar Wilde (1854 – 1900)

**What do I know about sex?
I'm a married man.**

- Tom Clancy (1947 –)

Familiarity breeds contempt – and children.

- Mark Twain (1835 – 1910)

**If I'm not in bed by eleven at night,
I go home.**

Henny Youngman (1906 – 1998)

Sex: The thing that takes up the least amount of time and causes the most amount of trouble.

- JOHN BARRYMORE (1882 – 1942)

The pleasure is momentary, the position ridiculous, and the expense damnable.

- LORD CHESTERFIELD (1694 – 1773)

Power is the ultimate aphrodisiac.

- HENRY KISSINGER (1923 –)

Is it not strange that desire should so many years outlive performance?

- WILLIAM SHAKESPEARE (1564 – 1616)

There are girls who manage to sell themselves, whom no one would take as a gift.

- NICOLAS CHAMFORT (1741 – 1794)

Remember if you smoke after sex, you're doing it too fast.

- WOODY ALLEN (1935 –)

Lust wants what it can't have.

Publilius Syrus (85 – 43 BC)

Immorality: the morality of those who are having a better time.

- H. L. Mencken (1880 – 1956)

Sex without love is an empty experience, but, as empty experiences go, it's one of the best.

- Woody Allen (1935 –)

Tell him I've been too fucking busy – or vice versa.

- DOROTHY PARKER (1893 – 1967)

To err is human – but it feels divine.

- MAE WEST (1893 – 1980)

My Dad told me "Anything worth having is worth waiting for." I waited until I was fifteen.

- ZSA ZSA GABOR (1917 –)

When choosing between two evils, I always like to take the one I've never tried before.

- MAE WEST (1893 – 1980)

The last time I was in a woman, I was visiting the Statue of Liberty.

- Woody Allen (1935 –)

Mae West

Dancing: A perpendicular expression of a horizontal desire.

- George Bernard Shaw (1856 – 1950)

A terrible thing happened to me last night – Nothing.

- Phyllis Diller (1917 – 2012)

Chapter 10

Love

Kind words can be short and easy to speak, but their echoes are truly endless.

- Mother Teresa (1910 – 1997)

The gods never let us love and be wise at the same time.

- Publilius Syrus (85 – 43 BC)

A woman has got to love a bad man once or twice in her life to be thankful for a good one.

- Marjorie Kinnan Rawlings (1896 – 1953)

We cannot really love anybody with whom we never laugh.

- Agnes Repplier (1855 – 1950)

Love is the triumph of imagination over intelligence.

- H. L. Mencken (1880 – 1956)

One is very crazy when in love.

- Sigmund Freud (1856 – 1939)

Love is a serious mental disease.

- Plato (424/423 – 348/347 BC)

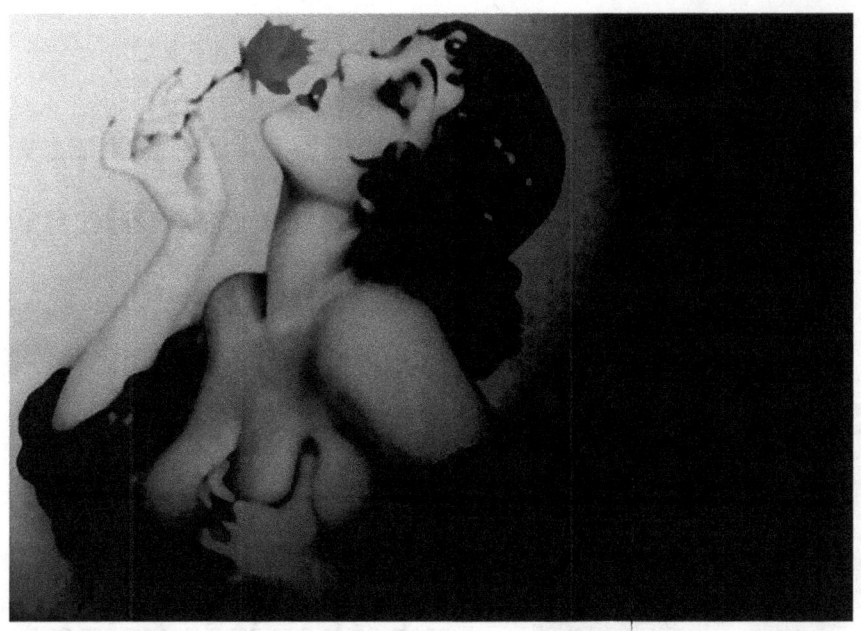

Great loves too must be endured.

- Coco Chanel (1883 – 1971)

Oh, what lies there are in kisses!

- Heinrich Heine (1797 – 1856)

Love is the state in which man sees things most decidedly as they are not.

- Friedrich Wilhelm Nietzsche (1844 – 1900)

Love takes up where knowledge leaves off.

- Thomas Aquinas (1225 – 1274)

Love: A temporary insanity curable by marriage.

- AMBROSE BIERCE (1842 – 1914)

Love is a fire. But whether it is going to warm your heart or burn down your house, you can never tell.

- JOAN CRAWFORD (1905 – 1977)

If two people love each other, there can be no happy end to it.

- ERNEST HEMINGWAY (1899 – 1961)

A fellow who sets out on love's road with an empty purse is taking on greater labors than Hercules.

- Titus Maccias Plautus (255 – 184 BC)

Love is the crocodile on the river of desire.

- Bhartrihari (6ᵀᴴ or 7ᵀᴴ Century)

First love is only a little foolishness and a lot of curiosity.

- George Bernard Shaw (1856 – 1950)

**I don't think anyone knows I love the girl;
I haven't done anything really silly yet.**

- Titus Maccius Plautus (255 – 184 BC)

**When two people love each other,
they don't look at each other, they look
in the same direction.**

- Ginger Rogers (1911 – 1995)

**What a woman says to a panting lover should
be written on the wind and running water.**

- Catullus (84 – 54 BC)

Love is the irresistible desire to be irresistibly desired.

- ROBERT FROST (1878 – 1963)

When we want to read of the deeds that are done for love whither do we turn? To the murder column.

- GEORGE BERNARD SHAW (1856 – 1950)

A woman loves you or she hates you; there's no other choice.

- PUBLILIUS SYRUS (85 – 43 BC)

Never go to bed mad. Stay up and fight.

- PHYLLIS DILLER (1917 – 2012)

Love is the delightful interval between meeting a beautiful girl and discovering that she looks like a haddock.

- John Barrymore (1882 – 1942)

There is always something ridiculous about the passions of people whom one has ceased to love.

- Oscar Wilde (1854 – 1900)

Love is the answer, but while you are waiting for the answer, sex raises some pretty good questions.

- Woody Allen (1935 –)

The average man is more interested in a woman who is interested in him than he is in a woman with beautiful legs.

- MARLENE DIETRICH (1901 – 1992)

In love, beauty counts for more than good advice.

- PUBLILIUS SYRUS (85 – 43 BC)

Look for a sweet person. Forget rich.

- ESTEE LAUDER (1908 – 2004)

Love is the greatest refreshment in life.

- Pablo Picasso (1881 – 1973)

No one is able to flee from death or love.

- Publilius Syrus (85 – 43 BC)

Love is a game that two can play and both win.

- Eva Gabor (1919 – 1995)

Christianity has done love a great service by making it a sin.

- Anatole France (1844 – 1924)

Men always want to be a woman's first love – women like to be a man's last romance.

- Oscar Wilde (1854 – 1900)

Women give men the very gold of their lives. But they invariably want it back in small change.

- Oscar Wilde (1854 – 1900)

Never forget that the most powerful force on earth is love.

- Nelson Rockefeller (1908 – 1979)

Chapter 11

Marriage

The husband who wants a happy marriage should learn to keep his mouth shut and his checkbook open.

- Groucho Marx (1890 – 1977)

Husbands are like fires. They go out if unattended.

- Zsa Zsa Gabor (1917 –)

Husbands never become good; they merely become proficient.

- H. L. Mencken (1880 – 1956)

My wife was too beautiful for words but not for arguments.

- JOHN BARRYMORE (1882 – 1942)

Woman begins by resisting a man's advances and ends by blocking his retreat.

- OSCAR WILDE (1854 – 1900)

Marriage is really tough because you have to deal with feelings and lawyers.

- RICHARD PRYOR (1940 – 2005)

THE PLEASURES OF THE COUNTRY.
SWEET HOME

"Home Sweet Home" must surely have been written by a bachelor.

- SAMUEL BUTLER (1835 – 1902)

By all means, marry. If you get a good wife, you'll become happy; if you get a bad wife, you'll become a philosopher.

- SOCRATES (470 – 399 BC)

Bachelors should be heavily taxed. It is not fair that some men should be happier than others.

- OSCAR WILDE (1854 – 1900)

> A woman usually respects her father, but her view of her husband is mingled with contempt, for she is, of course, privy to the transparent devices by which she snared him.
>
> - H. L. Mencken (1880 – 1956)

H. L. Mencken

> A dowry is a wonderful source of money, only if it comes without the wife.
>
> - Plautus (255 – 184 BC)

> American women expect to find in their husbands a perfection that English women only hope to find in their butlers.
>
> - W. Somerset Maugham (1874 – 1965)

I wonder if the screwing I'm getting is worth the screwing I'm getting.

- Lana Turner (1921 – 1995)

Marriage is a great institution but I'm not ready for an institution yet.

- Mae West (1893 – 1980)

Whenever you want to marry someone, go have lunch with his ex-wife.

- Shelley Winters (1920 – 2006)

I have learned that only two things are necessary to keep one's wife happy. First, let her think she's having her way, and second, let her have it.

- LYNDON B. JOHNSON (1908 – 1973)

Marriage is popular because it combines the maximum of temptation with the maximum of opportunity.

- GEORGE BERNARD SHAW (1856 – 1950)

The trouble with some women is that they get all excited about nothing – and then marry him.

- CHER (1946 –)

Hollywood brides keep the bouquets and throw away the grooms.

- GROUCHO MARX (1890 – 1977)

Bigamy is having one wife too many. Monogamy is the same.

- OSCAR WILDE (1854 – 1900)

We sleep in separate rooms, we have dinner apart, we take separate vacations – we're doing everything we can to keep our marriage together.

- RODNEY DANGERFIELD (1921 – 2004)

I wasn't always rich. There was a time I didn't know where my next husband was coming from.

- Mae West (1893 – 1980)

Paying alimony is like feeding hay to a dead horse.

- Grouch Marx (1890 – 1977)

You never realize how short a month is until you pay alimony.

- John Barrymore (1882 – 1942)

It's a funny thing that when a man hasn't anything on earth to worry about, he goes off and gets married.

- Robert Frost (1878 – 1963)

Brides aren't happy – they are just triumphant.

- John Barrymore (1882 – 1942))

A man's friends like him but leave him as he is – his wife loves him and is always trying to turn him into somebody else.

- G. K. Chesterton (1874 – 1936)

Marriage makes an end of many short follies – being one long stupidity.

- FRIEDRICH WILHELM NIETZSCHE (1844 – 1900)

Marriage: A friendship recognized by the police.

- ROBERT LOUIS STEVENSON (1850 – 1894)

Marriage is neither heaven nor hell, it is simply purgatory.

- ABRAHAM LINCOLN (1809 – 1865)

Of all men, Adam was the happiest; he had no mother-in-law.

- Mark Twain (1835 – 1910)

Marriage is the only adventure open to the cowardly.

- Voltaire (1694 – 1778)

Politics doesn't make strange bedfellows – marriage does.

- Groucho Marx (1890 – 1977)

Rich widows are the only secondhand goods that sell at first-class prices.

- Benjamin Franklin (1706 – 1790)

Conscience is a mother-in-law whose visit never ends.

- H. L. Mencken (1880 – 1956)

You don't know anything about a woman until you meet her in court.

- Norman Mailer (1923 – 2007)

Chapter 12

Women

When a woman speaks sweetly, she's plotting mischief.

- Florus (circa 53 – 138)

Women's styles may change but their designs remain the same.

- Oscar Wilde (1854 – 1900)

On one issue, at least, men and women agree: They both distrust women.

- H. L. Mencken (1880 – 1956)

Of all the wild beasts of land or sea, the wildest is women.

- MENANDER (342 – 291 BC)

Let thy maidservant be faithful, strong and homely.

- BENJAMIN FRANKLIN (1706 – 1790)

The way to fight a woman is with your hat. Grab it and run.

- JOHN BARRYMORE (1882 – 1942)

A woman is always buying something.

- Ovid (43 BC – AD 17)

Woman is surely the daughter of delay.

- Titus Maccius Plautus (255 – 184 BC)

When women kiss, it always reminds one of prize fighters shaking hands.

- H. L. Mencken (1880 – 1956)

As Miss America, my goal is to bring peace to the entire world and then to get my own apartment.

- Jay Leno (1950 –)

Better that a girl has beauty than brains, because boys see better than they think.

- Josh Billings (1818 – 1885)

I don't know anything better than a woman, if you want to spend money where it'll show.

- Frank McKinney "Kin" Hubbard (1868 – 1930)

Women would be more charming if one could fall into her arms without falling into her hands.

- AMBROSE BIERCE (1842 – 1914)

A woman talks to one man, looks at a second, and thinks of a third.

- BHARTRIHARI (6TH OR 7TH CENTURY)

Women are like elephants to me, I like to look at 'em but I wouldn't want to own one.

- W. L. FIELDS (1880 – 1946)

I do not know if she was virtuous, but she was ugly, and with a woman, that is half the battle.

- HEINRICH HEINE (1797 – 1856)

Her face was her chaperone.

- RUPERT HUGHES (1872 – 1956)

No cavalry or infantry has the gall to maneuver as coolly as a woman can.

- PLAUTUS (255 – 184 BC)

Good girls go to heaven, bad girls go everywhere.

- Helen Gurley Brown (1922 – 2012)

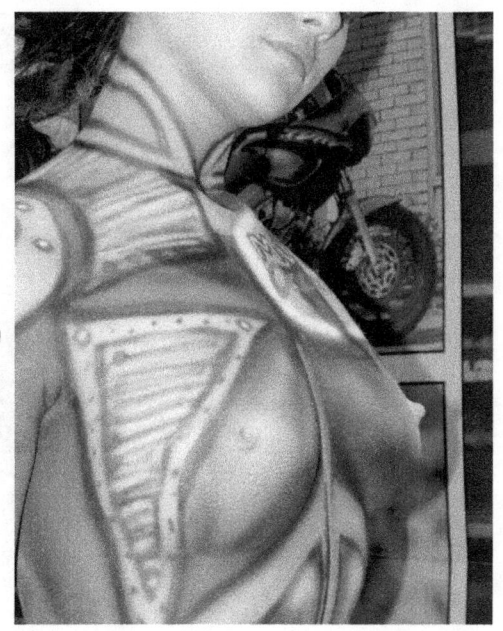

Who loves not women, wine, and song remains a fool his whole life long.

- Martin Luther (1483 – 1546)

In order to avoid being called a flirt, she always yielded easily.

- Charles Maurice De Talleyrand (1754 – 1838)

She's the kind of girl who climbed the ladder of success wrong by wrong.

- Mae West (1892 – 1980)

She got her good looks from her father. He's a plastic surgeon.

- Groucho Marx (1890 – 1977)

That woman speaks eighteen languages and she can't say "no" in any of them.

- Dorothy Parker (1893 – 1967)

**Gentlemen prefer blondes,
but take what they can get.**

- Don Herold (1889 – 1966)

**There is a lot to say in
her favor, but the other
is more interesting.**

- Mark Twain (1835 – 1910)

**Women should be observed
and not heard.**

- Groucho Marx (1890 – 1977)

**I'd rather have
two girls at 21 each
than one girl at 42.**

- W. C. Fields (1880 – 1946)

**Anyone who says he can
see through women
is missing a lot.**

- Groucho Marx (1890 – 1977)

**It's well to be off with
the old woman before
you're on with the new.**

- George Bernard Shaw (1856 – 1950)

Women are made to be loved, not understood.

- OSCAR WILDE (1854 – 1900)

Brains are an asset, if you hide them.

- MAE WEST (1892 – 1980)

If women didn't exist, all the money in the world would have no meaning.

- ARISTOTLE ONASSIS (1906 – 1975)

She's afraid that if she leaves, she'll become the life of the party.

- Groucho Marx (1890 – 1977)

If all these sweet young things were laid end to end, I wouldn't be the slightest bit surprised.

- Dorothy Parker (1893 – 1967)

She was what we used to call a suicide blonde – dyed by her own hand.

- Saul Bellow (1915 – 2005)

Chapter 13

Man

He is man, the most terrible of the beasts.

- G. K. Chesterton (1874 – 1936)

Man is a two-legged animal without feathers.

- Plato (424/423 – 348/347 BC)

I believe the best definition of man is the ungrateful biped.

- Fyodor Dostoyevsky (1821 – 1881)

It is even harder for the average ape to believe that he has descended from man.

- H. L. Mencken (1880 – 1956)

What an ugly beast is the ape, and how like us.

- Cicero (106 – 43 BC)

We need not worry so much about what man descends from – it's what he descends to that shames the human race.

- Mark Twain (1835 – 1910)

Who so would be a man must be a nonconformist.

- Ralph Waldo Emerson (1803 – 1882)

Man is a reasoning rather than a reasonable animal.

- Alexander Hamilton (1755 – 1804)

The civilized world represents the victory of persuasion over force.

- Plato (424/423 – 348/347 BC)

Man is the only animal that blushes. Or needs to.

- MARK TWAIN (1835 – 1910)

What men call . . . good fellowship is commonly but the virtue of pigs in a litter which lie close together to keep each other warm.

- HENRY DAVID THOREAU (1817 – 1862)

Good breeding consists of concealing how much we think of ourselves and how little we think of the other person.

- MARK TWAIN (1835 – 1910)

Don't overestimate the decency of the human race.

- H. L. Mencken (1880 – 1956)

All that I care to know is that a man is a human being – that is enough for me; he can't be any worse.

- Mark Twain (1835 – 1910)

I love mankind; it's people I can't stand.

- Charles Schulz "Peanuts" (1922 – 2000)

Histories are more full of examples of the fidelity of dogs than of friends.

- ALEXANDER POPE (1688 – 1744)

If you pick up a starving dog and make him prosperous, he will not bite you; that is the principal difference between a dog and a man.

- MARK TWAIN (1835 – 1910)

It is easier to denature plutonium than to denature the evil spirit of man.

- ALBERT EINSTEIN (1879 – 1955)

Man: The glory, jest and riddle of the world.

- ALEXANDER POPE (1688 – 1744)

You can't say civilization don't advance … in every war they kill you a new way.

- WILL ROGERS (1879 – 1935)

Men are moved by two levers only: fear and self-interest.

- NAPOLEON BONAPARTE (1769 – 1821)

Napoleon in Egypt

Civilization is a limitless multiplication of unnecessary necessities.

- Mark Twain (1835 – 1910)

Men have become the tools of their tools.

- Henry David Thoreau (1817 – 1862)

Things are in the saddle, and ride mankind.

- Ralph Waldo Emerson (1803 – 1882)

Those who hate vice, hate mankind.

- Pliny the Younger (61/63 – 113)

The earth has a skin, and that skin has diseases; one of its diseases is called man.

- Friedrich Wilhelm Nietzsche (1844 – 1900)

The most costly of all follies is to believe passionately in the palpably not true. It is the chief occupation of mankind.

- H. L. Mencken (1880 – 1956)

History teaches us that men and nations behave wisely once they have exhausted all other alternatives.

- Abba Eban (1915 – 2002)

This world is a comedy to those that think; a tragedy to those that feel.

- Horace Walpole (1717 – 1797)

Perhaps I know best why it is man alone who laughs: He alone suffers so deeply that he had to invent laughter.

- Friedrich Willhelm Nietzsche (1844 – 1900)

Adam was only human. He did not want the apple for the apple's sake; he wanted it only because it was forbidden.

- Mark Twain (1835 – 1910)

I sometimes think that God, in creating man, somewhat overestimated his ability.

- Oscar Wilde (1854 – 1900)

If mankind had created man, he would be ashamed of his performance.

- Mark Twain (1835 – 1910)

Maybe the world is another planet's hell.

- ALDOUS HUXLEY (1894 – 1963)

We are here and it is now. Further than that, all human knowledge is moonshine.

- H. L. MENCKEN (1880 – 1956)

He is a self-made man and worships his creator.

- JOHN BRIGHT (1811 – 1889)

CHAPTER 14
Children

A boy is, of all wild beasts, the most difficult to manage.

- PLATO (424/423 – 348/347 BC)

A child is a curly, dimpled lunatic.

- RALPH WALDO EMERSON (1803 – 1882)

Children today are tyrants. They contradict their parents, gobble their food and tyrannize their teachers.

- SOCRATES (470 – 399 BC)

**Insanity is hereditary;
you can get it from your children.**

- SAM LEVENSON (1911 – 1980)

**Insomnia: A contagious disease transmitted
from babies to parents.**

- IMMANUEL KANT (1724 – 1804)

**Parents of young children should realize
that few people, and maybe no one, will find
their children as enchanting as they do.**

- BARBARA WALTERS (1929 –)

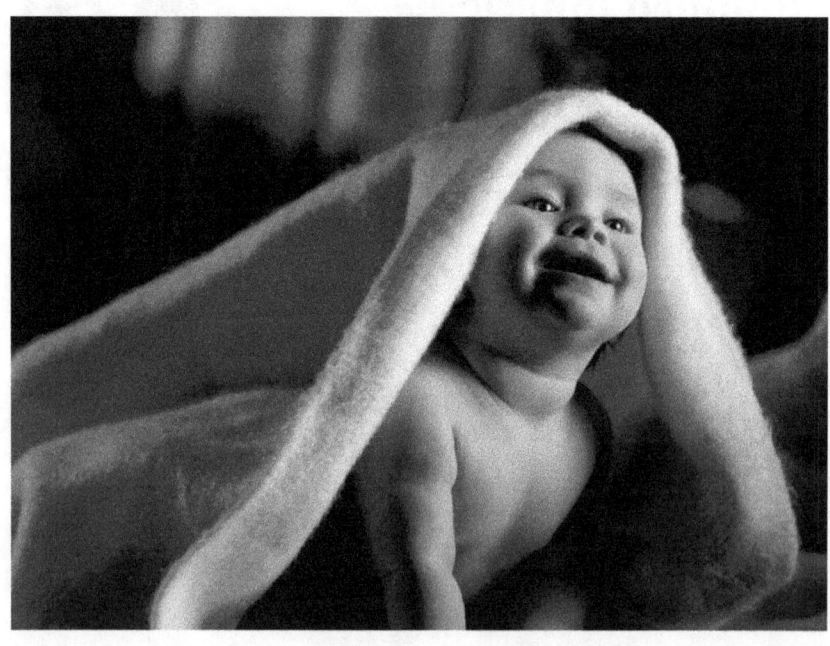

My mother had a great deal of trouble with me, but I think she enjoyed it.

- MARK TWAIN (1835 – 1910)

Children are given us to discourage our better emotions.

- H. H. MUNRO "SAKI" (1870 – 1916)

Never have children, only grandchildren.

- GORE VIDAL (1925 – 2012)

All God's children are not beautiful. Most of God's children are, in fact, barely presentable.

- Fran Lebowitz (1950 –)

We've been trying to have a kid. Well, she was trying, I just laid there.

- Bob Saget (1956 –)

Having children is like having a bowling alley installed in your brain.

- Martin Mull (1943 –)

The thing that impresses me about America is the way parents obey their children.

- DUKE OF WINDSOR (1894 – 1972)

When I was a boy of fourteen, my father was so ignorant I could hardly stand to have the old man around. But when I got to be 21, I was astonished at how much he had learned in seven years.

- MARK TWAIN (1835 – 1910)

Anyone who hates children and dogs can't be all bad.

- W. C. FIELDS (1880 – 1946)

Children make the most desirable opponents in Scrabble as they are both easy to beat and fun to cheat.

- Fran Lebowitz (1950 –)

A baby is an inestimable blessing and a bother.

- Mark Twain (1835 – 1916)

A happy childhood is poor preparation for human contact.

- Colette (1873 – 1954)

No matter how old a mother is, she watches her middle-aged children for signs of improvement.

- Florida Scott-Maxwell (1883 – 1979)

The best way to keep children at home is to make the atmosphere pleasant – and let the air out of the tires.

- Dorothy Parker (1893 – 1967)

Of children as of procreation - the pleasure momentary, the posture ridiculous, the expense damnable.

- Evelyn Waugh (1903 – 1966)

Children are never too tender to be whipped. Like tough beefsteaks, the more you beat them the more tender they become.

- Edgar Allan Poe (1809 – 1849)

I'm for bringing back the birch, but only for consenting adults.

- Gore Vidal (1925 –)

Little boys should be obscene and not heard.

- Oscar Wilde (1854 – 1900)

It is no wonder that people are so horrible when they start life as children.

- Kingsley Amis (1922 – 1995)

When I was kidnapped, my parents snapped into action. They rented out my room.

- Woody Allen (1935 –)

My eleven year old daughter mopes around the house all day, waiting for her breasts to grow.

- Bill Cosby (1937 –)

Never lend your car to anyone to whom you have given birth.

- ERMA BOMBECK (1927 – 1996)

My parents put a live teddy bear in my crib.

- WOODY ALLEN (1935 –)

My children didn't have my advantages; I was born into abject poverty.

- KIRK DOUGLAS (1916 –)

Providence protects children and idiots. I know because I have tested it.

- MARK TWAIN (1835 – 1910)

The first half of our life is ruined by our parents and the second half by our children.

- CLARENCE DARROW (1857 – 1938)

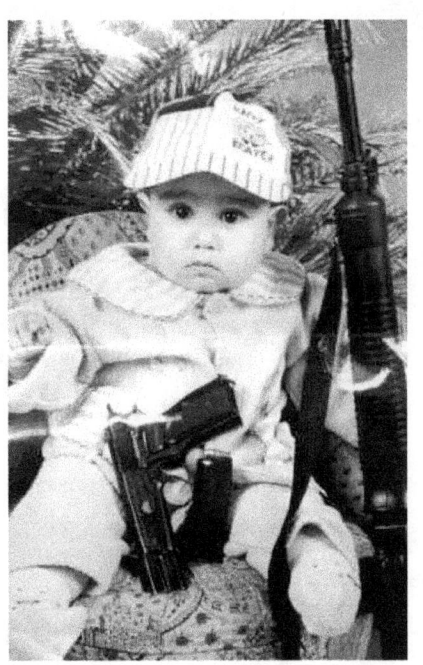

Like its politicians and its wars, society has the teenagers it deserves.

- J. B. PRIESTLEY (1894 – 1984)

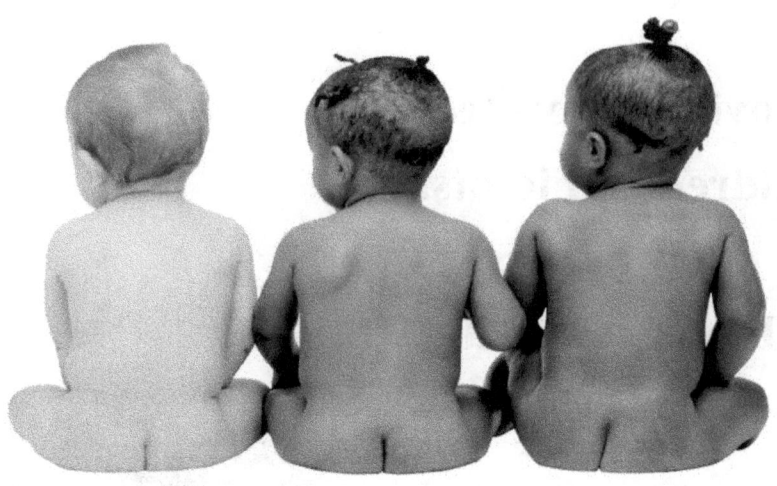

Sometimes, when I look at my children, I say to myself "Lillian, you should have stayed a virgin."

- Lillian Carter (1898 – 1983)
(Mother of President Jimmy Carter)

There are three terrible ages of childhood – 1 to 10, 10 to 20, 20 to 30.

- Cleveland Amory (1917 – 1998)

I could now afford all the things I never had as a kid, if I didn't have kids.

- Robert Orben (1927 –)

Chapter 15

Human Nature

A man who is not a fool can rid himself of every folly but vanity.

- Jean-Jacques Rousseau (1712 – 1778)

Most people would succeed in small things if they were not troubled by great ambitions.

- Henry Wadsworth Longfellow (1807 – 1882)

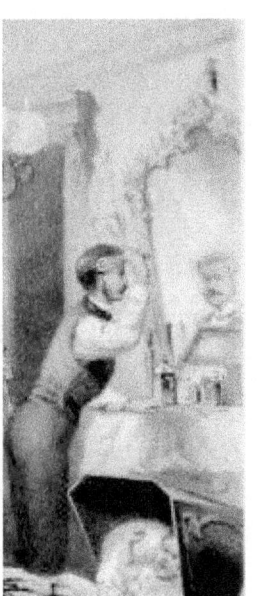

No luck is so good that you can't find some complaint.

- Publilius Syrus (85 – 43 BC)

Everyone thinks of changing the world but no one thinks of changing himself.

- Leo Tolstoy (1828 – 1910)

There are few who would not rather be hated than laughed at.

- Sydney Smith (1771 – 1845)

Nearly all men can stand adversity, but if you want to test a man's character, give him power.

- Abraham Lincoln (1809 – 1865)

We don't know what we want, but we are ready to bite somebody to get it.

- Will Rogers (1879 – 1935)

Will Rogers

It is a sin to believe evil of others, but it is seldom a mistake.

- H. L. Mencken (1880 – 1956)

Every generation laughs at the old fashions, but follows religiously the new.

- Henry David Thoreau (1817 – 1862)

Benjamin Franklin

He that falls in love with himself will have no rivals.

- BENJAMIN FRANKLIN (1706 – 1790)

In every work of genius we recognize our rejected thoughts.

- RALPH WALDO EMERSON (1803 – 1882)

The things that are hardest to bear are sweetest to remember.

- SENECA (54 BC – 39 AD)

> **What hurt him most was his outrageous opinion of his own worth.**
>
> - Cornelius Nepos (100 – 24 BC)

> **The trouble with most of us is that we would rather be ruined by praise than saved by criticism.**
>
> - Norman Vincent Peale (1898 – 1993)

> **Few things are harder to put up with than a good example.**
>
> - Mark Twain (1835 – 1910)

Shallow men believe in luck.

- George Bernard Shaw (1856 – 1950)

A good man is always a beginner.

- Martial (40 – 104)

Shallowness is natural; conceit comes with education.

- Cicero (106 – 43 BC)

It is easier to forgive an enemy than to forgive a friend.

- WILLIAM BLAKE (1757 – 1827)

Glory is fleeting, but obscurity is forever.

- NAPOLEON BONAPARTE (1769 – 1821)

Nobody ever forgets where he buried a hatchet.

- FRANK MCKINNEY "KIN" HUBBARD (1868 – 1930)

What a pleasant stain comes from an enemy's blood.

- Publilius Syrus (85 – 43 BC)

The hatred of relatives is the most violent.

- Tacitus (55 – 117)

I hold it better for the ruler to be feared than to be loved.

- Niccolò Machiavelli (1469 – 1527)

Few men have virtue to withstand the highest bidder.

- GEORGE WASHINGTON (1732 – 1799)

Most fools think they are only ignorant.

- BENJAMIN FRANKLIN (1706 – 1790)

Before a man speaks, it is always safe to assume that he is a fool. After he speaks, it is seldom necessary to assume it.

- H. L. MENCKEN (1880 – 1956)

Better a witty fool than a foolish wit.

- SHAKESPEARE (1564 – 1616)

What really flatters a man is that you think him worth flattering.

- GEORGE BERNARD SHAW (1856 – 1900)

Self-respect: the secure feeling that no one as yet is suspicious.

- H. L. MENCKEN (1880 – 1956)

Bore: A person who talks when you wish him to listen.

- AMBROSE BIERCE (1842 – 1914)

Bores bore each other too, but it never seems to teach them anything.

- DON MARQUIS (1878 – 1937)

We often forgive those who bore us, but we cannot forgive those whom we bore.

- FRANCOIS DE LA ROCHEFOUCAULD (1613 – 1680)

Gentlemen, you have just been listening to that Chinese sage, On Too Long.

- Will Rogers (1879 – 1935)

Bore: One who has the power of speech but not the capacity for conversation.

- Benjamin Disraeli (1804 – 1881)

The nice thing about being a celebrity is that when you bore people, they think it's their fault.

- Henry Kissinger (1923 –)

Tears for someone else's trouble dry quickly.

- CICERO (106 – 43 BC)

Men easily believe what they want to.

- CAESAR (100 – 44 BC)

A man's worst difficulties begin when he is able to do as he likes.

- THOMAS H. HUXLEY (1825 – 1895)

ADAM AND EVE IN THE GARDEN OF EDEN.

Chapter 16

Truth & Lies

There are only two ways of telling the complete truth – anonymously and posthumously.

- Thomas Sowell (1930 –)

Boys, I may not know much but I know chicken shit from chicken salad.

- Lyndon B. Johnson (1908 – 1973)

The fellow that agrees with everything you say is either a fool or he is getting ready to skin you.

- Frank McKinney "Kin" Hubbard (1868 – 1930)

The liar's punishment is not in the least that he is not believed but that he cannot believe anyone else.

- GEORGE BERNARD SHAW (1856 – 1950)

Bill Clinton

No man has a good enough memory to be a successful liar.

- ABRAHAM LINCOLN (1809 – 1865)

No one lies so boldly as the man who is indignant.

- FRIEDRICH WILHELM NIETZSCHE (1844 – 1900)

Get your facts first and then you can distort them as much as you please.

- Mark Twain (1835 – 1910)

When liars speak the truth, they are not believed.

- Aristotle (384 – 322 BC)

Honesty is a good thing, but it is not profitable to its possessor unless it is kept under control.

- Don Marquis (1878 – 1937)

If I were two-faced, would I be wearing this one?

- ABRAHAM LINCOLN (1809 – 1865)

Truth is beautiful – without doubt; but so are lies.

- RALPH WALDO EMERSON (1803 – 1882)

The pure and simple truth is rarely pure and never simple.

- OSCAR WILDE (1854 – 1900)

Actions lie louder than words.

- CAROLYN WELLS (1862 – 1942)

Honesty is the best image.

- TOM WILSON "ZIGGY" (1931 –)

We ought never to do wrong when people are looking.

- MARK TWAIN (1835 – 1910)

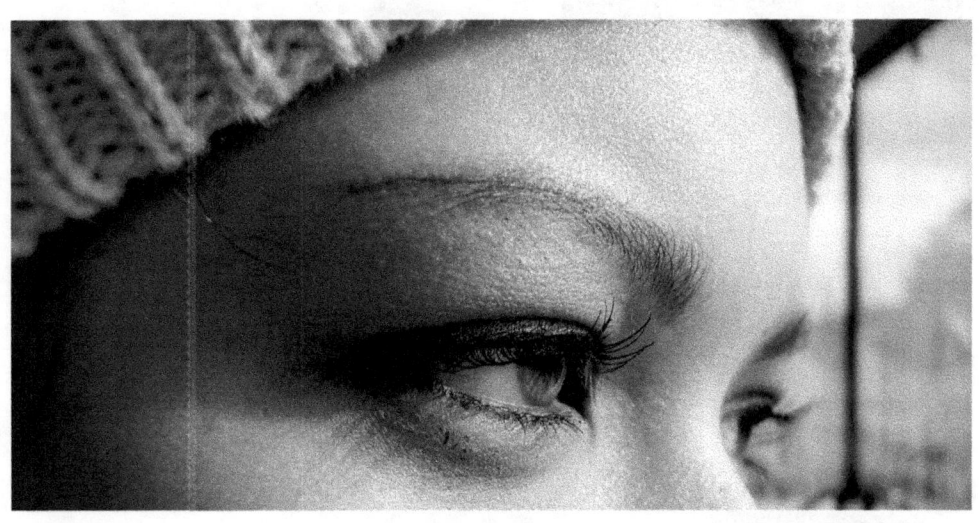

Confession may be good for my soul but it's bad for my reputation.

- MARK TWAIN (1835 – 1910)

A little inaccuracy sometimes saves tons of explanations.

- H. H. MUNRO "SAKI" (1870 – 1916)

Though I am not naturally honest, I am so sometimes by chance.

- SHAKESPEARE (1564 – 1616)

It is hard to believe a man is telling the truth when you know that you would lie if you were in his place.

- H. L. Mencken (1880 – 1956)

The Right Honorable Gentleman is indebted to his memory for his jests and his imagination for his facts.

- Richard Brinsley Sheridan (1751 – 1816)

A lie can run around the world six times while the truth is still trying to put on its pants.

- Mark Twain (1835 – 1910)

> **I never did give anybody hell. I just told the truth and they thought it was hell.**
>
> - Harry S. Truman (1884 – 1972)

> **As scarce as the truth is, the supply has always been in excess of the demand.**
>
> - Josh Billings (1818 – 1885)

> **Ye shall know the truth and the truth shall make you mad.**
>
> - Aldous Huxley (1894 – 1963)

Whatever deceives seems to produce a magical enchantment.

- Plato (424/423 – 348/347 BC)

The great masses of the people ... will more easily fall victims to a great lie than to a small one.

- Adolf Hitler (1889 – 1945)

Carlyle said "A lie cannot live"; it shows he did not know how to tell them.

- Mark Twain (1835 – 1910)

Joseph Stalin

The best way to keep one's word is not to give it.

- Napoleon Bonaparte (1769 – 1821)

Gaiety is the outstanding feature of the Soviet Union.

- Joseph Stalin (1878 – 1953)

Convictions are more dangerous foes of truth than lies.

- Friedrich Wilhelm Nietzsche (1844 – 1900)

When you read a biography, remember that the truth is never fit for publication.

- GEORGE BERNARD SHAW (1856 – 1950)

Winston Churchill

Men occasionally stumble over the truth, but most of them pick themselves up and hurry off as if nothing had happened.

- WINSTON CHURCHILL (1874 – 1965)

It is unfortunate, considering that enthusiasm moves the world, that so few enthusiasts can be trusted to speak the truth.

- ARTHUR BALFOUR (1848 – 1930)

The best mind-altering drug is truth.

- LILY TOMLIN (1939 –)

The least initial deviation from the truth is multiplied later a thousand fold.

- Aristotle (384 – 322 BC)

Most writers regard the truth as their most valuable possession, and therefore are most economical in its use.

- Mark Twain (1835 – 1910)

The difference between truth and fiction is that fiction has to make sense.

- Mark Twain (1835 – 1910)

A thing is not necessarily true because badly uttered, nor false because spoken magnificently.

- Saint Augustine (354 – 430)

CHAPTER 17

Politicians

A politician is an animal who can sit on a fence and keep both ears to the ground.

- H. L. Mencken (1880 – 1956)

A politician is a person with whose politics you don't agree; if you agree with him, he is a statesman.

- David Lloyd George (1863 – 1945)

Politicians are interested in people. Not that this is always a virtue. Fleas are interested in dogs.

- P. J. O'Rourke (1947 –)

Ninety percent of politicians give the other ten percent a bad name.

- Henry Kissinger (1923 –)

Nine politicians out of ten are knaves who maintain themselves by preying on the idiotic vanities and pathetic hopes of half-wits.

- H. L. Mencken (1880 – 1956)

Politicians are the same all over: They promise to build a bridge even when there is no river.

- Nikita Khrushchev (1894 – 1971)

Those who are too smart to engage in politics are punished by being governed by those who are dumber.

- Plato (424/423 – 348/347 BC)

He knows nothing and he thinks he knows everything. That points clearly to a political career.

- George Bernard Shaw (1856 – 1950)

If a politician found he had cannibals among his constituents, he would promise them missionaries for dinner.

- H. L. Mencken (1880 – 1956)

You can fool too many of the people too much of the time.

- JAMES THURBER (1894 – 1961)

With Congress, every time they make a joke, it's a law, and every time they make a law, it's a joke.

- WILL ROGERS (1879 – 1935)

The function of socialism is to raise suffering to a higher level.

- NORMAN MAILER (1923 - 2007)

If presidents don't do it to their wives, they do it to the country.

- MEL BROOKS (1926 -)

**In order to become the master,
the politician poses as the servant.**

- CHARLES DE GAULLE (1890 – 1970)

**The secret of the demagogue is to make
himself as stupid as his audience so that
they believe they are as clever as he.**

- KARL KRAUS (1874 – 1936)

Your public servants serve you right.

- ADLAI STEVENSON (1900 – 1965)

Now and then an innocent man is sent to the legislature.

- Frank McKinney "Kin" Hubbard (1868 – 1930)

There is no act of treachery or meanness of which a political party is not capable; for in politics there is no honor.

- Benjamin Disraeli (1804 – 1881)

Mothers all want their sons to grow up to be president but they don't want them to become politicians in the process.

- John F. Kennedy (1917 – 1963)

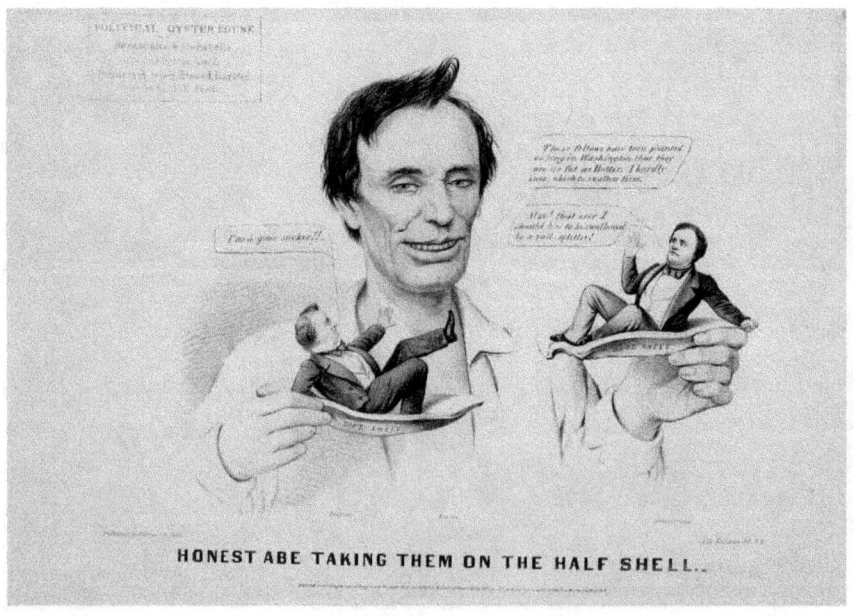

During an election campaign, the air is full of speeches and vice versa.

- Henry Adams (1838 – 1918)

In America you can go on the air and kid the politicians, and the politicians can go on the air and kid the people.

- Groucho Marx (1890 – 1977)

Nothing is so admirable in politics as a short memory.

- John Kenneth Galbraith (1908 – 2006)

Since a politician never believes what he says, he is surprised when others believe him.

- Charles de Gaulle (1890 – 1970)

Politics is far more complicated than physics.

- Albert Einstein (1879 – 1955)

Oh, that lovely title, Ex-president.

- Dwight D. Eisenhower (1890 – 1969)

Communism, like any other revealed religion, is largely made up of prophecies.

- H. L. Mencken (1880 – 1956)

I would not like to be a political leader in Russia. They never know when they're being taped.

- RICHARD NIXON (1913 – 1994)

Richard Nixon

In politics, an absurdity is not a handicap.

- NAPOLEON BONAPARTE (1769 – 1821)

The first mistake in public business is going into it.

- BENJAMIN FRANKLIN (1706 – 1790)

I got fed up with all the sex and sleaze and backhanders of rock'n'roll, so I went into politics.

- Tony Blair (1953 –)

The more you observe politics, the more you've got to admit that each party is worse than the other.

- Will Rogers (1879 – 1935)

Their insatiable lust for power is only equaled by their incurable impotence in exercising it.

- Winston Churchill (1874 – 1965)

Vilify! Vilify! Some of it will always stick.

- Pierre Augustin Beaumarchais (1732 – 1799)

The popularity of a bad man is as treacherous as he is himself.

- PLINY THE YOUNGER (62 –113)

The best political community is formed by citizens of the middle class and those states are likely to be well administered in which the middle class is large and larger if possible than both the other classes … or at any rate than either singly.

- ARISTOTLE (384 – 322 BC)

Men hesitate less to injure a man who makes himself loved than to injure one who makes himself feared.

- NICCOLÒ MACHIAVELLI (1469 – 1527)

Chapter 18
Democracy

Democracy is the theory that the common people know what they want, and deserve to get it good and hard.

- H. L. Mencken (1880 – 1956)

Democracy substitutes election by the incompetent many for appointment by the corrupt few.

- George Bernard Shaw (1856 – 1950)

Under democracy, one party always devotes its chief energies to trying to prove that the other party is unfit to rule – and both commonly succeed, and are right.

- H. L. Mencken (1880 – 1956)

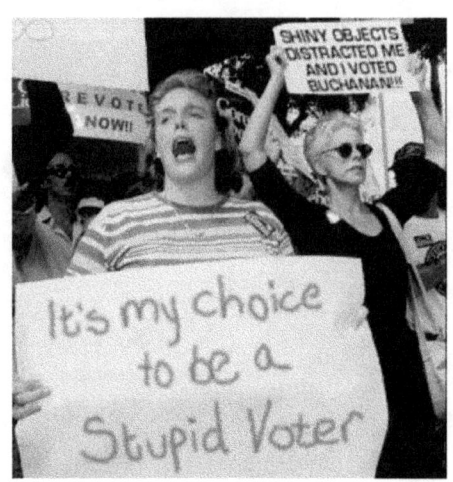

Democracy gives every man the right to be his own oppressor.

- JAMES RUSSELL LOWELL (1819 – 1891)

Democracy is a process by which the people are free to choose the men who will get the blame.

- LAURENCE J. PETER (1919 – 1990)

The whole dream of democracy is to raise the proletarian to the level of stupidity attained by the bourgeois.

- GUSTAVE FLAUBERT (1821 – 1880)

Man's capacity for justice makes democracy possible, but man's inclination to injustice makes democracy necessary.

- REINHOLD NIEBUHR (1892 – 1971)

Giving every man a vote has no more made men wise and free than Christianity has made them good.

- H. L. MENCKEN (1880 – 1956)

In general, the art of government consists in taking as much money as possible from one class of citizens to give to the other.

- VOLTAIRE (1694 – 1778)

It is dangerous to be right when the government is wrong.

- Voltaire (1694 – 1778)

The urge to save humanity is almost always a false front for the urge to rule.

- H. L. Mencken (1880 – 1956)

What luck for rulers that men do not think.

- Adolf Hitler (1889 – 1945)

The pleasure of governing must certainly be exquisite if we may judge from the vast numbers who are eager to be concerned with it.

- Voltaire (1694 – 1778)

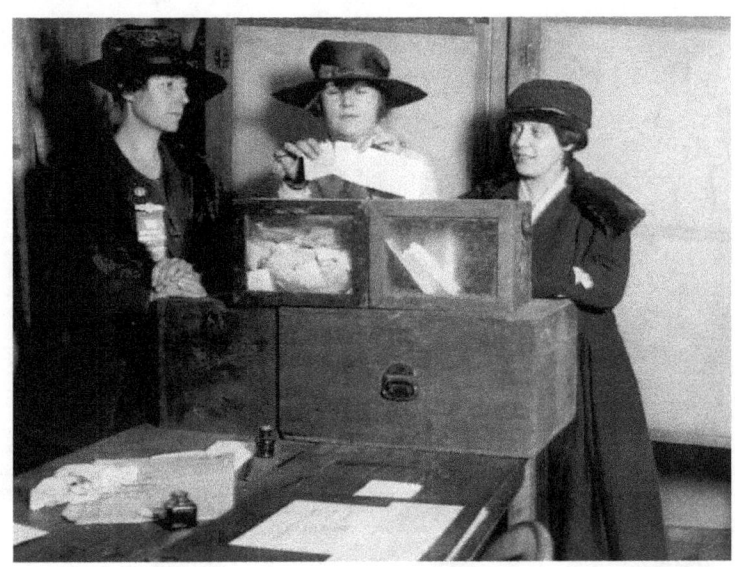

The trouble with free elections is you never know who is going to win.

- LEONID BREZHNEV (1906 – 1982)

I don't make jokes. I just watch the government and report the facts.

- WILL ROGERS (1879 – 1935)

When there is no middle class, and the poor greatly exceed in number, troubles arise and the state soon comes to an end.

- ARISTOTLE (384 – 322 BC)

Republics end through luxury, monarchy through poverty.

- Montesquieu (1689 – 1755)

That government is best which governs least.

- Henry David Thoreau (1817 – 1862)

Government has no other end but the preservation of property.

- John Locke (1632 – 1704)

I disapprove of what you say, but I will defend to the death your right to say it.

- Voltaire (1694 – 1778)

I know of no example in time or place of a society that has been marked by a large measure of political freedom, and that has not also used something comparable to a free market.

- Milton Friedman (1912 – 2006)

Those who expect to reap the blessings of freedom must, like men, undergo the fatigue of supporting it.

- Thomas Paine (1737 – 1809)

People demand freedom of speech as a compensation for the freedom of thought which they seldom use.

- Soren Aabye Kierkegaard (1813 – 1855)

It is amazing how wise statesmen can be when it is ten years too late.

- DAVID LLOYD GEORGE (1863 – 1945)

Sincere diplomacy is no more possible than dry water.

- JOSEPH STALIN (1878 – 1953)

The more law, the less justice.

- CICERO (106 – 43 BC)

When you say that you agree to a thing in principle you mean that you have not the slightest intention of carrying it out.

- OTTO VON BISMARCK (1815 – 1898)

The law is reason free from passion.

- Aristotle (384 – 322 BC)

If you like laws and sausages, you should never watch either one being made.

- Otto Von Bismarck (1815 – 1898)

The government solution to a problem is usually as bad as the problem.

- Milton Friedman (1912 – 2006)

In rivers and bad governments, the lightest things swim at the top.

- BENJAMIN FRANKLIN (1706 – 1790)

"MONKEY SHINES."

A government is the only known vessel that leaks from the top.

- JAMES RESTON (1909 – 1995)

I'd rather entrust the government of the United States to the first four hundred people listed in the Boston telephone directory than to the faculty of Harvard University.

- WILLIAM F. BUCKLEY, JR. (1925 – 2008)

Fleas can be taught nearly everything a congressman can.

- MARK TWAIN (1835 – 1910)

The difference between bad speech and bad deeds is opportunity.

- MARCUS FABIUS QUINTILIANUS (35 – 100)

Creative semantics is the key to contemporary government; it consists of talking in strange tongues lest the public learn the inevitable inconveniently early.

- GEORGE WILL (1941 –)

Chapter 19

Religion

A casual stroll through the lunatic asylum shows that faith does not prove anything.

- Friedrich Wilhelm Nietzsche (1844 – 1900)

Faith must trample under foot all reason, sense and understanding.

- Martin Luther (1483 – 1546)

The way to see by faith is to shut the eye of reason.

- Benjamin Franklin (1706 – 1790)

Everyone prefers belief to the exercise of judgment.

- Seneca (54 BC – 39 AD)

Religion is a conceited effort to deny the most obvious realities.

- H. L. Mencken (1880 – 1956)

A cult is a religion with no political power.

- Tom Wolfe (1931 –)

If God did not exist it would have been necessary to invent Him.

- Voltaire (1694 – 1778)

The impotence of God is infinite.

- Anatole France (1844 – 1924)

Man rarely (if ever) manages to dream up a god superior to themselves. Most gods have the manners of a spoiled child.

- Robert A. Heinlein (1907 – 1988)

A Sunday School is a prison in which children do penance for the evil conscience of their parents.

- H. L. Mencken (1880 – 1956)

There is something feeble and a little contemptible about a man who cannot face the perils of life without the help of comfortable myths.

- Bertrand Russell (1872 – 1970)

When a man is freed of religion, he has a better chance to live a normal and wholesome life.

- Sigmund Freud (1856 – 1939)

The worshiper is the father of the gods.

- H. L. Mencken (1880 – 1956)

Which is it, is man one of God's blunders or is God one of man's?

- Friedrich Wilhelm Nietzsche (1844 – 1900)

It takes a long while for a naturally trustful person to reconcile himself to the idea that after all God will not help him.

- H. L. Mencken (1880 –1956)

God, that dumping ground of our dreams.

- Jean Rostand (1894 – 1977)

The average man does not know what to do with his life, yet wants another one which will last forever.

- Anatole France (1844 – 1924)

Say what you will about the Ten Commandments, you must always come back to the pleasant fact that there are only ten of them.

- H. L. Mencken (1880 – 1956)

Men enriched by your sweat and misery, made you superstitious not that you might fear God, but that you might fear them.

- VOLTAIRE (1694 – 1778)

Religion is excellent stuff for keeping common people quiet.

- NAPOLEON BONAPARTE (1769 – 1821)

Science has done more for the development of Western civilization in one hundred years than Christianity did in eighteen hundred years.

- JOHN BURROUGHS (1837 – 1921)

Christianity must be divine, since it has lasted 1,700 years, despite the fact that it is so full of villainy and nonsense.

- Voltaire (1694 – 1778)

There is not enough religion in the world to destroy the world's religions.

- Friedrich Wilhelm Nietzsche (1844 – 1900)

Unless you hate your father and mother and wife and brothers and sisters and yes, even you own life, you can't be my disciple.

- Jesus Christ (7-2 BC – 26-36 AD) Luke 14:26

So far as I can remember, there is not one word in the Gospels in praise of intelligence.

- BERTRAND RUSSELL (1872 – 1970)

The inspiration of the Bible depends on the ignorance of the gentlemen who read it.

- ROBERT G. INGERSOLL (1833 – 1899)

It ain't those parts of the Bible that I can't understand that bother me, it's the parts that I do understand.

- MARK TWAIN (1835 – 1910)

**We have just enough religion
to make us hate, but not enough
to make us love one another.**

- JONATHAN SWIFT (1667 – 1745)

**Puritanism: The haunting fear that
someone, somewhere, may be happy.**

- H. L. MENCKEN (1880 – 1956)

**The Catholic faith is confession
on Saturday. Absolution on Sunday.
At it again on Monday.**

- H. G. WELLS (1866 – 1946)

God is always on the side of the big battalions.

- Voltaire (1694 – 1778)

Christian theology is not only opposed to the scientific spirit; it is opposed to every other form of rational thinking.

- H. L. Mencken (1880 – 1956)

The age of ignorance commenced with the Christian system.

- Thomas Paine (1737 – 1809)

The first clergyman was the first rascal who met the first fool.

- VOLTAIRE (1694 – 1778)

Next to a circus, there ain't nothing that packs up and tears out of town any quicker than the Christmas spirit.

- FRANK MCKINNEY "KIN" HUBBARD (1868 – 1930)

When I hear a man preach, I like to see him act as if he were fighting bees.

- ABRAHAM LINCOLN (1809 – 1865)

CHAPTER 20

Death

Don't go to sleep, so many people die there.

- MARK TWAIN (1835 – 1910)

If this is dying, then I don't think much of it.

- LYTTON STRACHEY (1880 – 1932)

I don't want to achieve immortality through my work. I want to achieve it through not dying.

- WOODY ALLEN (1935 –)

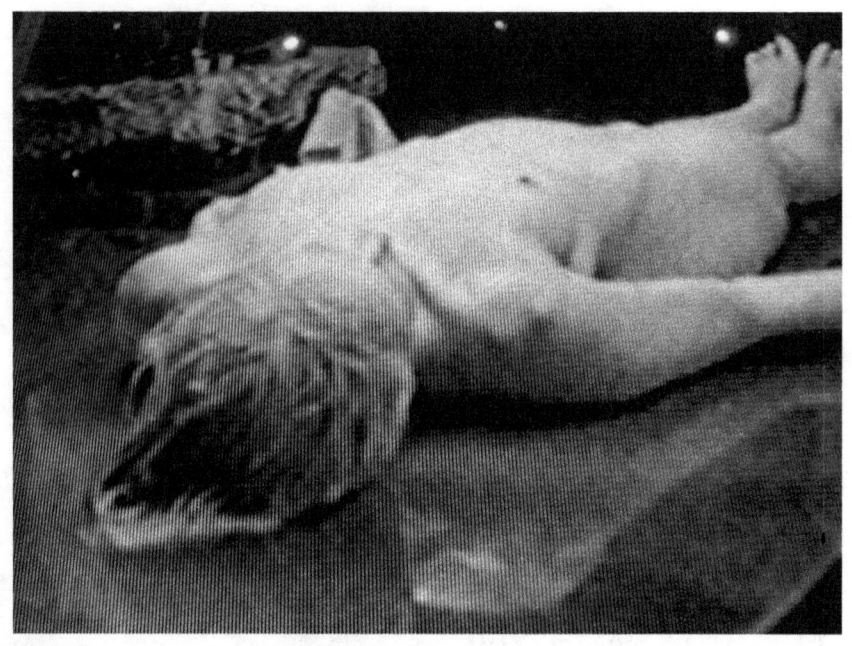

**The reports of my death
are greatly exaggerated.**

- Mark Twain (1835 – 1910)

**They say such nice things about people at
their funerals that it makes me sad to realize
that I'm going to miss mine by just a few days.**

- Garrison Keillor (1942 –)

**A cynic is a man who when he smells flowers
looks around for a coffin.**

- H. L. Mencken (1880 – 1956)

I know a man who gave up smoking, drinking, sex, and rich food. He was healthy right up to the time he killed himself.

- Johnny Carson (1925 – 2005)

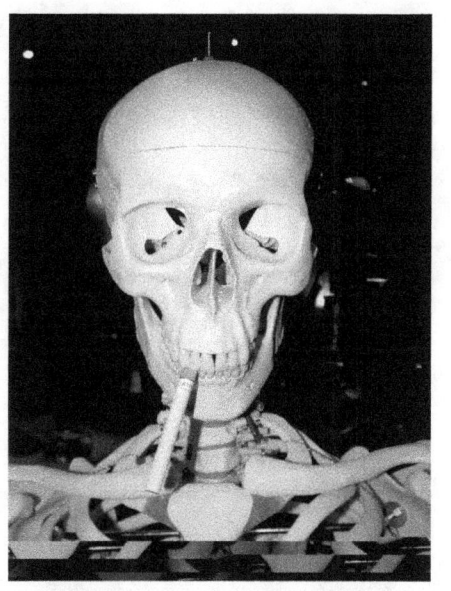

I have a fine heart … it will last me as long as I live.

- W. C. Fields (1880 – 1946)

I take my only exercise acting as pallbearer at the funerals of my friends who exercise regularly.

- Mark Twain (1835 – 1910)

It's not that I'm afraid to die. I just don't want to be there when it happens.

- Woody Allen (1935 –)

I refused to attend his funeral. But, I wrote a nice letter explaining that I approved of it.

- Mark Twain (1835 – 1910)

If Roosevelt were alive today, he'd turn over in his grave.

- Samuel Goldwyn (1882 – 1974)

You need religion if you are terrified of death.

- GORE VIDAL (1925 – 2012)

I don't believe in an after life, although I am bringing a change of underwear.

- WOODY ALLEN (1935 –)

I am ready to meet my Maker. Whether my Maker is ready to meet me is another matter.

- WINSTON S. CHURCHILL (1874 – 1965) ON HIS 75TH BIRTHDAY

> **Don't let it end like this. Tell them I said something.**
>
> - Pancho Villa (1878 – 1923)
> Last words

> **Let us endeavor so to live that when we come to die even the undertaker will be sorry.**
>
> - Mark Twain (1835 – 1910)

> **There is nothing more exhilarating than to be shot at without results.**
>
> - Winston Churchill (1874 – 1965)

When you have to kill a man, it costs nothing to be polite.

- WINSTON CHURCHILL (1874 – 1965)

One murder makes a villain; millions, a hero.

- NAPOLEON BONAPARTE (1769 – 1821)

A single death is a tragedy. A million deaths is a statistic.

- JOSEPH STALIN (1878 – 1953)

**If fame is to come only after death,
I am in no hurry for it.**

- Martial (40 – 104)

**Murderer: One presumed to be innocent
until declared insane.**

- Oscar Wilde (1854 – 1900)

**The only completely consistent
people are the dead.**

- Aldous Huxley (1894 – 1963)

**No matter how much
a woman loved a man,
it would still give her
a glow to see him commit
suicide for her.**

- H. L. Mencken (1880 – 1956)

**Suicide is belated
acquiescence in the
opinion of one's wife's
relatives.**

- H. L. Mencken (1880 – 1956)

**The thought of suicide is
a great consolation: with
the help of it, one has got
through many a bad night.**

- Friedrich Wilhelm Nietzsche (1844 – 1900)

The disciples of a martyr suffer much more than the martyr.

- Friedrich Wilhelm Nietzsche (1844 – 1900)

A thing is not necessarily true because a man dies for it.

- Oscar Wilde (1854 – 1900)

Martyrdom covers a multitude of sin.

- Mark Twain (1835 – 1910)

Epitaph: An inscription on a tomb, showing that virtues acquired by death have a retroactive effect.

- Ambrose Bierce (1842 – 1914)

If you take epitaphs seriously, we ought to bury the living and resurrect the dead.

- Mark Twain (1835 – 1910)

ACTUAL EPITAPHS:

Excuse my dust.

- Dorothy Parker (1893 – 1967)

The rarest quality in an epitaph is truth.

- Henry David Thoreau (1817 – 1862)

Pardon me for not getting up.

- Ernest Hemingway (1899 – 1961)

On the whole, I'd rather be in Philadelphia.

- W. C. Fields (1880 – 1946)

I'm involved in a plot.

- Alfred Hitchcock (1899 – 1980)

Chapter 21

Youth & Aging

Youth is a wonderful thing. What a crime to waste it on children.

- GEORGE BERNARD SHAW (1856 – 1950)

In America, the young are always to give to those who are older than themselves the full benefit of their inexperience.

- OSCAR WILDE (1854 – 1900)

Blessed are the young, for they shall inherit the national debt.

- HERBERT HOOVER (1874 – 1964)

There is no sadder sight than a young pessimist, except an old optimist.

- MARK TWAIN (1835 – 1910)

W. Somerset Maugham

I suppose it's difficult for the young to realize that one may be old without being a fool.

- W. SOMERSET MAUGHAM (1874 – 1965)

The young always have the same problem – how to rebel and conform at the same time. They have now resolved this by defying their parents and copying one another.

- QUENTIN CRISP (1908 – 1999)

Men are like wine, some turn to vinegar, the best improve with age.

- POPE JOHN XXIII (1881 – 1963)

At age fifty, every man has the face he deserves.

- GEORGE ORWELL (1903 – 1950)

No wise man ever wished to be younger.

- JONATHAN SWIFT (1667 – 1745)

> We do not count
> a man's years until he
> has nothing else
> to count.
>
> - Ralph Waldo Emerson
> (1803 – 1882)

> … of age, that age
> appears to be best in
> four things – old wood
> best to burn, old wine
> to drink, old friends
> to trust, and old
> authors to read.
>
> - Francis Bacon (1561 – 1626)

> It is unbecoming
> for young men
> to utter maxims.
>
> - Aristotle (384 – 322 BC)

A man is as old as the woman he feels.

- Groucho Marx (1890 – 1977)

I am not young enough to know everything.

- Oscar Wilde (1854 – 1900)

**I'm pushing sixty.
That is enough exercise for me.**

- Mark Twain (1835 – 1910)

Young men want to be faithful and are not; old men want to be faithless and cannot.

- OSCAR WILDE (1854 – 1900)

After fifty, a man begins to deteriorate, but in the forties, he is at the maximum of his villainy.

- H. L. MENCKEN (1880 – 1956)

If I'd known I was gonna live this long, I'd have taken better care of myself.

- EUBIE BLAKE (1887 – 1983)

As long as a woman can look ten years younger than her own daughter, she is perfectly satisfied.

- Oscar Wilde (1854 – 1900)

Man weeps to think that he will die so soon; woman that she was born so long ago.

- H. L. Mencken (1880 – 1956)

Time and tide wait for no man, but time always stands still for a woman of thirty.

- Robert Frost (1878 – 1963)

The secret of staying young is to live honestly, eat slowly, and lie about your age.

- Lucille Ball (1911 – 1989)

When people tell you how young you look, they are also telling you how old you are.

- Cary Grant (1904 – 1986)

After age seventy, it's patch, patch, patch.

- Jimmy Stewart (1908 – 1997)

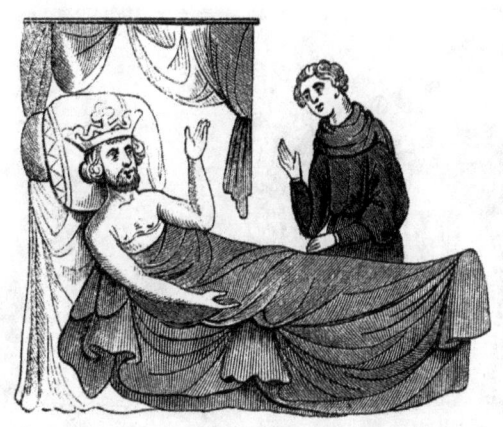

From birth to age 18, a girl needs good parents. From 18 to 35, she needs good looks. From 35 to 55, she needs a good personality. From 55 on, she needs good cash.

- Sophie Tucker (1884 – 1996)

The old believe everything, the middle-aged suspect everything, the young know everything.

- Oscar Wilde (1854 – 1900)

No one is so old as not to think he can live one more year.

Cicero (106 – 43 BC)

When a woman gets too old to be attractive to man, she turns to God.

- Honorè de Balzac (1799 – 1850)

Youth had been a habit of hers for so long that she could not part with it.

- Rudyard Kipling (1865 – 1936)

It is after you have lost your teeth that you can afford to buy steaks.

Pierre Auguste Renoir (1841 – 1919)

Wrinkles should merely indicate where smiles have been.

- Mark Twain (1835 – 1910)

Old age is like a plane flying through a storm. Once you are aboard, there is nothing you can do.

- Golda Meir (1898 – 1978)

To get back my youth, I would do anything in the world, except take exercise, get up early or be respectable.

- Oscar Wilde (1854 – 1900)

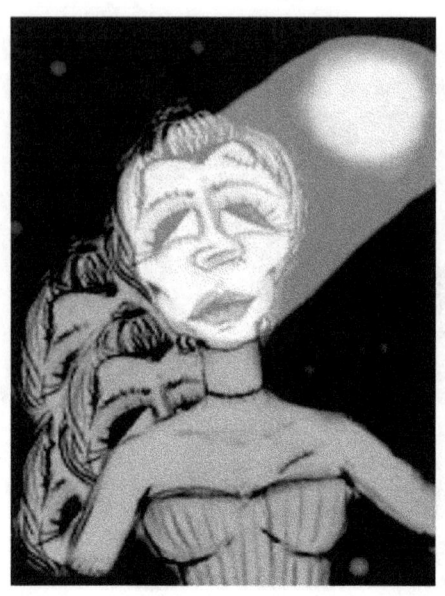

One should never trust a woman who tells one her real age. A woman who would tell one that would tell one anything.

- Oscar Wilde (1854 – 1900)

Retirement at sixty five is ridiculous. When I was sixty five, I still had pimples.

- George Burns (1896 – 1996)

You know you're getting old when the candles cost more than the cake.

- Bob Hope (1903 – 2003)

Chapter 22

Life & Happiness

The art of living is more like wrestling than dancing.

- Marcus Aurelius (121 – 180)

Life does not cease to be funny when people die any more than it ceases to be serious when people laugh.

- George Bernard Shaw (1856 – 1950)

Life is an effort that deserves a better cause.

- Karl Kraus (1874 – 1936)

Life itself is the proper binge.

- Julia Child (1912 – 2004)

If I had to live my life again,
I'd make the same mistakes, only sooner.

- Tallulah Bankhead (1902 – 1968)

There are two tragedies in life. One is to lose your heart's desire. The other is to gain it.

- George Bernard Shaw (1856 – 1950)

Life can only be understood backwards, but it must be lived forward.

- Soren Kierkegaard (1813 – 1855)

Life is a constant oscillation between the sharp horns of a dilemma.

- H. L. Mencken (1880 – 1956)

The good life is one inspired by love and guided by knowledge.

- Bertrand Russell (1872 – 1970)

There is no cure for birth and death, save to enjoy the interval.

- George Santayana (1863 – 1952)

We must laugh at man to avoid crying for him.

- Napoleon Bonaparte (1769 – 1821)

To be stupid, selfish and have good health are three requirements for happiness.

- Gustave Flaubert (1821 – 1880)

The unexamined life is not worth living.

- Socrates (470 – 399 BC)

The longer I live, the more beautiful life becomes.

- Frank Lloyd Wright (1867 – 1959)

Life would be infinitely happier if we could only be born at the age of eighty and gradually approach eighteen.

- Mark Twain (1835 – 1910)

**Mistakes are part of the dues
one pays for a full life.**

- Sophia Loren (1934 –)

**We are always getting ready to live,
but never living.**

- Ralph Waldo Emerson (1803 – 1882)

**The basic fact about human existence is not
that it is a tragedy, but it is a bore.**

- H. L. Mencken (1880 – 1956)

**Start every day with a smile –
and get it over with.**

- W. C. Fields (1880 – 1946)

**Always do right. That will gratify some
of the people and astonish the rest.**

- Mark Twain (1835 – 1910)

**Life is much too important a thing
to talk seriously about it.**

- Oscar Wilde (1854 – 1900)

It is not reason which is the guide to life, but custom.

- DAVID HUME (1711 – 1776)

Men can only be happy when they do not assume that the object of life is happiness.

- GEORGE ORWELL (1903 – 1950)

Happiness is not something you experience, it's something you remember.

- OSCAR LEVANT (1906 – 1972)

It is neither wealth nor splendor, but tranquility and occupation which give happiness.

- Thomas Jefferson (1743 – 1826)

The greater part of our happiness or misery depends on our dispositions and not on our circumstances.

- Martha Washington (1731 – 1802)

If only we'd stop trying to be happy, we could have a pretty good time.

- Edith Wharton (1862 – 1937)

The secret of being miserable is to have the leisure to bother about whether you are happy or not.

- GEORGE BERNARD SHAW (1856 – 1950)

Happy is he who causes scandal.

- SALVADOR DALI (1904 – 1989)

Amusement is the happiness of those who cannot think.

- ALEXANDER POPE (1688 – 1744)

Grief can take care of itself; but to get the full value of a joy, you must have somebody to divide it with.

- Mark Twain (1835 – 1910)

Birds sing after a storm; why shouldn't people feel as free to delight in whatever remains to them?

- Rose Kennedy (1890 – 1995)

Youth is a blunder, manhood a struggle, old age a regret.

- Benjamin Disraeli (1804 – 1881)

The trouble with life is that there are so many beautiful women and so little time.

- John Barrymore (1882 – 1942)

Life being what it is, one dreams of revenge.

- Paul Gauguin (1848 – 1903)

Life is a dead end street.

- H. L. Mencken (1880 – 1956)

APPENDIX

Biographies

The purpose of these biographies is to give a quick background on the people who are quoted. Most of the names are familiar. Dozens of scholarly volumes have been written about many of these public figures. These biographies in no way do justice to their lives, careers or contributions to mankind. As a quick, fun reference, I hope it is useful.

All biographies come from Wikipedia, the free encyclopedia, unless otherwise referenced.

Adams, Henry Brooks

Henry Brooks Adams (February 16, 1838 – March 27, 1918) was an American novelist, journalist, historian and academic. He is best-known for his autobiographical book, *The Education of Henry Adams*. He was a member of the Adams political family.

Ade, George

George Ade (February 9, 1866 – May 16, 1944) was an American writer, newspaper columnist, and playwright.

Ade was born in Kentland, Indiana. In 1890 Ade joined the *Chicago Morning News*, which later became the *Chicago Record*. He wrote the column, *Stories of the Streets and of the Town*. In the column, George Ade illustrated Chicago life. It featured characters like Artie, an office boy; Doc Horne, a gentlemanly liar; and Pink Marsh, a black shoeshine boy. Ade's well-know "fables in slang" also made their first appearance in this popular column.

Adenauer, Konrad

Konrad Hermann Josef Adenauer (January 5, 1876 – April 19, 1967) was a German statesman. Although his political career spanned 60 years, beginning as early as 1906, he is most noted for his role as the first Chancellor of West Germany from 1949 – 1963 and chairman of the Christian Democratic Union from 1950 to 1966. He was the oldest chancellor ever to serve Germany, leaving at the age of 87.

Ali, Muhammad

Muhammad Ali (born **Cassius Marcellus Clay, Jr**. on January 17, 1942) is a retired American boxer, former three-time World Heavyweight Champion, and winner of an Olympic Light-heavyweight gold medal. In 1999, Ali was crowned "Sportsman of the Century" by *Sports Illustrated* and the BBC.

Allen, Fred

Fred Allen (born **John Florence Sullivan** on May 31, 1894 in Cambridge, Massachusetts, died March 17, 1956 in New York City) was an American comedian whose absurdist, pointed radio show (1934 – 1949) made him one of the most popular and forward-looking humorists in the so-called classic era of American radio.

His best-remembered gag may be his long-running mock feud with friend and fellow comedian Jack Benny. Allen has been considered one of the more accomplished, daring and relevant humorists of his time. A master ad libber, he constantly battled censorship and developed routines the style and substance of which influenced future comic talents, notably Stan Freberg. Perhaps more than any of his generation, Fred Allen wielded influence that outlived both his contemporaries and the medium that made him famous.

Allen, Woody

Woody Allen (born **Allen Stewart Königsberg** on December 1, 1935) is a four-time Academy Award-winning American film director, writer, actor, jazz musician, comedian and playwright. His large body of work and cerebral film style, mixing satire, wit and humor, have made him one of the most respected and prolific filmmakers in the modern era. Allen writes and directs his movies and has also acted in the majority of them. For inspiration, Allen draws heavily on literature, sexuality, philosophy, psychology, Judaism, European cinema and New York City, where he was born and has lived his entire life.

Amis, Kingsley

Sir Kingsley William Amis, CBE (April 16, 1922 – October 22, 1995) was an English novelist, poet, critic, and teacher. He wrote more than twenty novels, three collections of poetry, short stories, radio and television scripts, and books of social and literary criticism. He fathered English novelist Martin Amis.

Amory, Cleveland

Cleveland Amory (September 2, 1917 – October 14, 1998) was an American author who devoted his life to promoting animal rights. He was perhaps best known for his books about his cat named *Polar Bear*, whom he saved from the New York streets on Christmas Eve, 1978.

Aquinas, Thomas

Thomas Aquinas, O.P. (also **Saint Thomas Aquinas**, **Thomas of Aquin**, or **Aquino**; c. 1225 – 7 March 1274) was an Italian Catholic priest in the Dominican Order, a philosopher and theologian in the scholastic tradition, known as **Doctor Angelicus, Doctor Universalis** and **Doctor Communis.** He was the foremost classical proponent of natural theology, and the father of the Thomistic school of philosophy and theology.

Aristotle

Aristotle (Greek: 'Ἀριστοτέλης Aristotélēs) (384 BC – 322 BC) was a Greek philosopher, a student of Plato and teacher of Alexander the Great. He wrote on many different subjects, including physics, metaphysics, poetry, theater, music, logic, rhetoric, politics, government, ethics, biology and zoology. Aristotle (together with Socrates and Plato) is one of the most important philosophers in Western thought. He was

one of the first to systematize philosophy and science. His thinking on physics and science had a profound impact on medieval thought, which lasted until the Renaissance, and the accuracy of some of his biological observations was only confirmed in the last century. His logical works contain the earliest formal study of logic that we have, which was not superseded until the late nineteenth century. In the Middle Ages, Aristotelian metaphysics had a profound influence on philosophical and theological thinking in the Islamic and Jewish traditions, and on Christian thought, where its legacy is still felt in Christian theology, for example in Orthodox theology, and especially within the Catholic tradition shaped by scholasticism. All aspects of Aristotle's philosophy continue to be the object of active academic study today

Augustine of Hippo

Aurelius Augustinus, Augustine of Hippo, or **Saint Augustine** (November 13, 354 – August 28, 430) was a philosopher and theologian, and was bishop of the North African city of Hippo Regius for the last third of his life. Augustine is one of the most important figures in the development of Western Christianity, and is considered to be one of the church fathers. He framed the concepts of original sin and just war.

Aurelius, Marcus

Marcus Aurelius Antoninus Augustus (Rome, April 26, 121 – Vindobona or Sirmium, March 17, 180) was Roman Emperor from 161 to his death in 180. He was the last of the "Five Good Emperors", and is also considered one of the most important stoic philosophers.

His tenure was marked by wars in Asia against a revitalized Parthian Empire, and with Germanic tribes along the *Limes Germanicus* into Gaul and across the Danube. A revolt in the East, led by Avidius Cassius, failed.

Marcus Aurelius' work *Meditations*, written on campaign between 170 – 180, is still revered as a literary monument to a government of service and duty and has been praised for its "exquisite accent and its infinite tenderness."

Bacall, Lauren

Betty Jane Perske (born September 16, 1924), better known as **Lauren Bacall**, is a Golden Globe– and Tony Award–winning, as well as Academy Award–nominated, American film and stage actress and model. Known for her husky voice and sultry looks, she became a famous icon in the 1940s and has kept on acting to this day.

She is perhaps best known for being a film noir leading lady in films such as *The Big Sleep* (1946) and *Dark Passage* (1947), as well as a comedienne, as seen in 1953's *How to Marry a Millionaire*. Bacall also enjoyed success starring in the Broadway musicals *Applause* in 1970 and *Woman of the Year* in 1981.

Bacon, Francis

Francis Bacon, 1st Viscount St Alban (22 January 1561 – 9 April 1626) was an English philosopher, statesman, and essayist. He is also known as a proponent of the scientific revolution. Indeed, according to John Aubrey, his dedication may have brought him into a rare historical group of scientists who were killed by their own experiments.

His works established and popularized an inductive methodology for scientific inquiry, often called the *Baconian method* or simply, the scientific method. In the context of his time such methods were connected with the occult trends of hermeticism and alchemy. Nevertheless, his demand for a planned procedure of investigating all things natural marked a new turn in the rhetorical and theoretical framework for science, much of which still informs conceptions of proper methodology today.

Baez, Joan

Joan Chandos Baez (born January 9, 1941) is an American folk singer and songwriter known for her highly individual vocal style. She is a soprano with a three-octave vocal range and a distinctively rapid vibrato. Many of her songs are topical and deal with social issues.

She is best known for her hits "There But For Fortune", "Diamonds & Rust" and "The Night They Drove Old Dixie Down", and to a lesser extent, "We Shall Overcome", "Love Is Just A Four-Letter

Word", "Farewell Angelina", "Sweet Sir Galahad", and "Joe Hill" (songs she performed at the 1969 Woodstock festival).

Balfour, Arthur

Arthur James Balfour, 1st Earl of Balfour, KG, OM, PC (25 July 1848 – 19 March 1930) was a British Conservative politician and statesman, and the Prime Minister from 1902 to 1905, a time when his party and government became divided over the issue of tariff reform. Later, as Foreign Secretary, he authored the Balfour Declaration of 1917, which supported the establishment of a Jewish homeland in Palestine.

Ball, Lucille

Lucille Désirée Ball (August 6, 1911 – April 26, 1989) was an iconic American, comedienne, actress, glamour girl and star of the landmark sitcoms *I Love Lucy*, *The Lucy Show*, and *Here's Lucy*. Lucille Ball is one of the American's favorite stars and had one of Hollywood's longest careers. She was a major movie star from the 1930s to the 1970s, and appeared on television for more than 30 years. She won 13 Emmy Awards (more than any other person ever), and dozens of Golden Globes and Lifetime Achievement Awards. She was also nominated dozens of other times for Emmys and Golden Globes.

Balzac, Honoré de

Honoré de Balzac (May 20, 1799 – August 18, 1850) was a nineteenth-century French novelist and playwright. His magnum opus was a sequence of almost 100 novels and plays collectively entitled *La Comédie humaine*, which presents a panorama of French life in the years after the fall of Napoléon Bonaparte in 1815.

Due to his keen observation of detail and unfiltered representation of society, Balzac is regarded as one of the founders of realism in European literature. He is renowned for his multi-faceted characters; even his lesser characters are complex, morally ambiguous and fully human.

Bankhead, Tullulah

Tallulah Brockman Bankhead (January 31, 1902 – December 12, 1968) was an American actress, talk-show host and *bonne vivante*.

Bankhead was born in Huntsville, Alabama. She has been described as "an extremely homely child", overweight and with a deep, husky voice resulting from chronic bronchitis.

Bankhead came from a powerful Democratic political family in the South in general and Alabama in particular. Her father was the Speaker of the United States House of Representatives from 1936 – 1940. She was the niece of Senator John H. Bankhead II, and granddaughter of Senator John H. Bankhead. Bankhead herself was a Democrat, albeit one of a more liberal stripe than the rest of her family.

Her family sent her to various schools in an attempt to keep her out of trouble. At 15, Bankhead won a movie-magazine beauty contest and convinced her family to let her move to New York. She quickly won bit parts, first appearing in a non-speaking role in *The Squab Farm*. During these early New York years, she became a peripheral member of the Algonquin Round Table and known as a hard-partying girl-about-town.

In 1923, she made her debut on the London stage. She returned to the U.S. in 1931 to be Paramount Pictures' "next Marlene Dietrich", but Hollywood success eluded her in her first four films of the 1930s. Critics agree that her acting was flat, that she was unable to dominate the camera, and that she was generally outclassed by Dietrich, Carole Lombard, and others. She rented a home at 1712 Stanley Street, in Hollywood, and began hosting parties that were said to "have no boundaries". On September 9, 1932, she was featured on the cover of *Film Weekly*.

Bankhead's first film was *Tarnished Lady* (1931), directed by George Cukor, and Cukor and Bankhead became fast friends. Bankhead behaved herself on the set and filming went smoothly, but she found filmmaking to be very boring and didn't have the patience for it. She didn't like Hollywood either. When she met producer Irving Thalberg, she asked him, "How do you get laid in this dreadful place?"

Barber, Jerry

Carl Jerome "Jerry" Barber (April 25, 1916 – September 23, 1994) was a professional golfer on the PGA Tour.

He was born in Jacksonville, Illinois. Among his seven tour victories, Barber won the 1961 PGA Championship at Olympia Fields Country Club (a location not far from where Barber grew up) on the strength of one of the most astonishing displays of clutch putting in major championship history. Trailing Don January by four shots with three holes to play in the final round, Barber made a 20-foot birdie putt at the 16th hole, a 40-foot par-saving putt at 17, and a 60-foot birdie putt at 18 to tie January and force a playoff, which Barber won the next day by one stroke. Barber played on two Ryder Cup teams, 1955 and 1961, and also was team captain in 1961.

Barkley, Alben W.

Alben William Barkley (November 24, 1877 – April 30, 1956) was a Democratic member of the U.S. House of Representatives and the United States Senate from Paducah, Kentucky, and the thirty-fifth Vice President of the United States.

Barnum, P. T.

Phineas Taylor Barnum (July 5, 1810 – April 7, 1891) was an American showman who is best remembered for his entertaining hoaxes and for founding the circus that eventually became the Ringling Bros. and Barnum & Bailey Circus. Barnum never flinched from his stated goal "to put money in his own coffers". He was a businessman above all else, his profession was pure entertainment, and he was perhaps the first "show business" millionaire. He never said "There's a sucker born every minute" as is famously ascribed, but his rebuttal to his critics was often "I am a showman by profession…and all the gilding shall make nothing else of me." Although famous for his brazen self-promotion and blatant puffery, he understood his times and profited from them brilliantly.

Barry, Dave

David Barry, Jr. (born July 3, 1947) is a best selling American author and Pulitzer Prize-winning humorist who wrote a nationally syndicated column for the Miami Herald from 1983 to 2005.

Barrymore, John

John Sidney Blyth Barrymore (February 15, 1882 in Philadelphia, Pennsylvania – May 29, 1942 in Los Angeles, California) was an American actor.

He gained fame as a stage actor, lauded for his portrayals of Hamlet and Richard III, and is frequently called the greatest actor of his generation. He was the brother of Lionel Barrymore and Ethel Barrymore, and the grandfather of Drew Barrymore.

Beaumarchais, Pierre

Pierre-Augustin Caron de Beaumarchais (January 24, 1732 – May 17 – 18, 1799) was a watchmaker, inventor, musician, politician, invalid, fugitive, spy, publisher, arms dealer, and revolutionary (both French and American). He was best known, however, for his theatrical works, especially the three Figaro plays.

Behan, Brendan

Brendan Francis Behan (Irish: *Breandán Ó Beaucháin*) (February 9, 1923 – March 20, 1964) was an Irish poet, short story writer, novelist and playwright who wrote in both Irish and English. He was also a committed Irish Republican and an erstwhile member of the Irish Republican Army.

Behan was one of the most successful Irish dramatists of the 20th century.

Bellow, Saul

Saul Bellow, born Solomon Bellows (Lachine, Quebec, Canada, June 10, 1915 – April 5, 2005 in Brookline, Massachusetts), was an acclaimed Canadian-born American writer. He won the Nobel Prize in Literature in 1976 and the National Medal of Arts in 1988.

Bellow is best known for writing novels that investigate isolation, spiritual dissociation, and the possibilities of human awakening. Bellow drew inspiration from Chicago, his hometown, and he set much of his fiction there. His works exhibit a mix of high and low culture, and his fictional characters are also a potent mix of intellectual dreamers and street-smart confidence men. While on a Guggenheim fellowship in Paris, he wrote his best-known novel, *The Adventures of Augie March* (1953).

Bentham, Jeremy

Jeremy Bentham (26 February 1748 – 6 June 1832) was an English jurist, philosopher, and legal and social reformer. He was a political radical and a leading theorist in Anglo-American philosophy of law. He is best known for his advocacy of utilitarianism and his opposition to the concept of natural rights with oft quoted statements to the effect that such rights were nonsense. He influenced the development of welfarism.

Berenson, Bernard

Bernard Berenson (born June 26, 1865 in Butrimonys (now Vilna), Lithuania – October 6, 1959 in Florence, Italy) was an American art historian specializing in the Renaissance. He was a major figure in establishing the market for paintings by the Old Masters.

Berra, Yogi

Lawrence Peter "Yogi" Berra (born May 12, 1925 in St. Louis, Missouri) is a former Major League Baseball player and manager. He played almost his entire career for the New York Yankees and was elected to the baseball Hall of Fame in 1972. He was one of only four players to be named the Most Valuable Player of the American League three times, and one of only six managers to lead both American and National League teams to the World Series.

Berra, who quit school in the eighth grade, has a tendency toward malapropism and fracturing the English language in highly provocative, interesting ways. Simultaneously denying and confirming his reputation, Berra once stated, "I never said half the things I really said."

Bhartrihari

Bhartrihari is the name of a sixth or seventh century Sanskrit grammarian, and of a Sanskrit poet of roughly the same period. It is not known whether the two are identical.

Bierce, Ambrose

Ambrose Gwinett Bierce (June 24, 1842 – 1914(?)) was an American editorialist, journalist, short-story writer and satirist, today best known for his *Devil's Dictionary*.

Bierce's lucid, unsentimental style has kept him popular when many of his contemporaries have been consigned to oblivion. His dark, sardonic views and vehemence as a critic earned him the nickname, "**Bitter Bierce**". Such was his reputation that it was said his judgment on any piece of prose or poetry could make or break a writer's career. Among the younger writers whom he encouraged were the poet George Sterling and the fiction writer W. C. Morrow.

Billings, Josh

Josh Billings was the pen name of the humorist born **Henry Wheeler Shaw** (20 April 1818 – 14 October 1885). He was perhaps the second most famous humor writer and lecturer in the United States in the second half of the 19th century after Mark Twain, although his reputation has not fared so well with later generations.

Bismarck, Otto von

Otto Eduard Leopold von Bismarck, 1st Graf von Bismarck-Schönhausen, 1st Herzog von Lauenburg, 1st Fürst von Bismarck (born April 1, 1815 in Schönhausen, today Saxony-Anhalt; died July 30, 1898 in Friedrichsruh near Hamburg), was a Prussian and German statesman of the 19th century. As Minister-President of Prussia from 1862 – 90, he engineered the unification of Germany. From 1867 on, he was Chancellor of the North German Confederation. When the second German Empire was declared in 1871, he served as its first Chancellor, gaining the nickname "**Iron Chancellor**".

Bismarck held conservative monarchical views in the tradition of Klemens von Metternich, the Austrian statesman who devised the diplomatic arrangements which governed Europe after the Napoleonic Wars – arrangements which Bismarck upset. Bismarck's primary objectives were to ensure the supremacy of the Prussian state within Central Europe, and of the aristocracy within the state itself. His most significant achievement was the creation of the modern German state, with Prussia at its core, through a series of wars and political maneuvering in the 1860s. The final act, the Franco-Prussian War of 1870 – 71, saw Prussia break France's power on the European continent.

Blair, Tony

Anthony Charles Lynton Blair (born 6 May 1953) is a British politician who served as Prime Minister of the United Kingdom from 2 May 1997 to 27 June 2007. He was leader of the Labour Party from 1994 to 2007 and Member of Parliament for Sedgefield from 1983 to 2008. On the day he stood down as Prime Minister, he was appointed official Envoy of the Quartet on the Middle East on behalf of the United Nations, the European Union, the United States and Russia, and stepped down as an MP.

Blake, Eubie

James Hubert Blake (February 7, 1887 – February 12, 1983) was a composer, lyricist, and pianist of ragtime, jazz, and popular music. With long time collaborator Noble Sissle, Blake wrote the Broadway musical *Shuffle Along* in 1921; this was one of the first Broadway musicals ever to be written and directed by African Americans. Blake's compositions included such hits as, "Bandana Days", "Charleston Rag", ":Love Will Find A Way", "Memories of You", and "I'm Just Wild About Harry". The musical *Eubie!,* which featured the collective works of Blake, opened on Broadway in 1978.

Blake, William

William Blake (November 28, 1757 – August 12, 1827) was an English poet, painter, and printmaker. Largely unrecognized during his lifetime, Blake's work is today considered seminal and significant in the history of both poetry and the visual arts. He was voted 38th in a poll of the 100 Greatest Britons organized by the BBC in 2002.

Blount, Jr., Roy

Roy Alton Blount, Jr. (born October 4, 1941, in Indianapolis, Indiana) is an American writer. Best known as a humorist, Blount is also a reporter, actor, and musician with the Rock Bottom Remainders, a rock band composed entirely of writers. Blount graduated from Decatur High School in Decatur, Georgia, where he was editor of the school newspaper, *The Scribbler*, and Vanderbilt University. Recently he guided American television audiences down the Mississippi River, narrating the documentary *The Main Stream* for PBS. As of 2007 he is featured regularly as a panelist on the NPR news/comedy quiz show, *Wait Wait... Don't Tell Me*. On the show, Blount is known for outrageous deadpan comments which frequently reduce the panel to tears of laughter, such as his discussion of "E.J. Junior Senior Junior High School".

Bonaparte, Napoleon

Napoleon I (born **Napoleone di Buonaparte**, later **Napoléon Bonaparte**) (15 August 1769 – 5 May 1821) was a French military and political leader who had significant impact on modern European history. He was a general during the French Revolution, the ruler of France as First Consul (*Premier Consul*) of the French Republic, Emperor of the French (*Empereur des Français*), King of Italy, Mediator of the Swiss Confederation and Protector of the Confederation of the Rhine.

Bombeck, Erma

Erma Louise Bombeck (February 21, 1927 – April 22, 1996), born **Erma Fiste**, was an American humorist who achieved great popularity for a newspaper column that depicted suburban home life in the second half of the 20th century.

Born in Dayton, Ohio, Bombeck graduated from the University of Dayton in 1949 with a degree in English. She started her career in 1949 as a reporter for the Dayton Journal Herald, but after marrying school administrator Bill Bombeck, a college friend, she left the job and raised three children.

As the children grew she started writing *At Wit's End*, telling self-deprecating tales about the life of a housewife. It debuted in the *Kettering-Oakwood Times* in 1964. She was paid $3 per column.

Growing popularity led *At Wit's End* to be nationally syndicated in 1965, and eventually it ran three times a week in more than 700 newspapers. The column was collected in many best-selling books, and her fame was such that a television sitcom was based on her. The series, *Maggie*, ran for eight shows in 1982 before being cancelled.

Boorstin, Daniel J.

Daniel Joseph Boorstin (October 1, 1914 – February 28, 2004) was a prolific American historian, professor, attorney, and writer. He served as the U.S. Librarian of Congress from 1975 until 1987.

Brando, Marlon

Marlon Brando, Jr. (April 3, 1924 – July 1, 2004) was an Academy Award-winning American actor whose body of work spanned over half a century. He is widely regarded as one of the most influential actors of all time. Brando is best known for his roles in *A Streetcar Named Desire* and *On the Waterfront*, both directed by Elia Kazan in the early 1950s, as well as his Academy-Award winning performance as Vito Corleone in *The Godfather* and as Colonel Walter E. Kurtz in *Apocalypse Now*, the latter two directed by Francis Ford Coppola in the 1970s. Brando also garnered worldwide attention by playing Jor-El in *Superman: The Movie* (1978), directed by Richard Donner.

Brezhnev, Leonid

Leonid Ilyich Brezhnev (December 19, 1906 – November 10, 1982) was General Secretary of the Communist Party of the Soviet Union (and thus political leader of the USSR) from 1964 to 1982, serving in that position longer than anyone other than Joseph Stalin. He was twice Chairman of the Presidium of the Supreme Soviet (head of state), from 1960 to 1964 and from 1977 to 1982.

Bright, John

John Bright (November 16, 1811 – March 27, 1889), Quaker, was a British Radical and Liberal statesman, associated with Richard Cobden in the formation of the Anti-Corn Law League. He was one of the greatest orators of his generation, and a strong critic of British foreign policy.

Brooks, Mel

Mel Brooks (born June 28, 1926) is a multi-award winning American director, writer, comedian, actor and producer best known as a creator of broad film farces and comedy parodies. Brooks is a member of the short list of entertainers with the distinction of having won an Emmy, a Grammy, an Oscar and a Tony award.

Brown, Helen Gurley

Helen Gurley Brown (February 18, 1922 in Green Forest, Arkansas – August 13, 2012 in New York City), was an author, publisher, and businesswoman. She was editor-in-chief of *Cosmopolitan* magazine for 32 years. In 1962, at the age of 40, Brown authored the best selling book Sex and the Single Girl. In 1965 she became editor-in-chief of Cosmopolitan and reversed the fortunes of the failing magazine. During the decade of the 1950s she was an outspoken advocate of women's sexual freedom and sought to provide them with role models and a guide in her magazine. Brown claimed that women could have it all, "love, sex, and money". Due to her advocacy, the liberated single woman was often referred to generically as the "Cosmo Girl". Her work played a part in what is often called the sexual revolution.

Buckley, Jr., William F.

William Frank "Bill" Buckley, Jr. (November 24, 1925 – February 27 2008) was an American author and conservative commentator. He founded the political magazine *National Review* in 1955, hosted the television show *Firing Line* from 1966 until 1999, and was a nationally syndicated newspaper columnist. His writing style was famed for its eloquence, wit, and use of uncommon words. Over the course of his career, Buckley's views changed on some issues, such as drug legalization, which he came to favor. In his December 1, 2007 column, Buckley claimed to favor banning tobacco.

Buckley was the author of a series of novels featuring the character of CIA agent Blackford Oakes, along with dozens of other books on writing, speaking, history, politics, and sailing. Buckey referred to himself "on and off" as either libertarian or conservative. He was based in New York City and Stamford, Connecticut. Buckley often signed his name as "**WFB.**"

Burns, George

George Burns (born **Nathan Birnbaum** January 20, 1896 – March 9, 1996) was an Academy Award-winning Jewish-American comedian and actor.

His career spanned vaudeville, film, radio, and television, with and without his equally legendary wife, Gracie Allen. His arched eyebrow and cigar smoke punctuation became familiar trademarks for over three quarters of a century. Enjoying a remarkable career resurrection that began at age 79, and ended shortly before his death at age 100, George Burns was as well known in the last two decades of his life as at any other time during his career.

Burroughs, John

John Burroughs (April 3, 1837 – March 29, 1921) was an American naturalist and essayist important in the evolution of the U.S. conservation movement. According to biographers at the American Memory project at the Library of Congress, John Burroughs was the most important practitioner after Thoreau of that especially American literary genre, the nature essay. By the turn of the century he had become a virtual cultural institution in his own right: the Grand Old Man of Nature at a time when the American romance with the idea of nature, and the American conservation movement, had come fully into their own.

His extraordinary popularity and popular visibility were sustained by a prolific stream of essay collections, beginning with *Wake-Robin* in 1871.

Burton, Richard

Richard Burton, CBE (November 10, 1925 – August 5, 1984) was a Welsh actor. He was at one time the highest-paid actor in Hollywood. Known for his distinctive voice, he was nominated seven times for Academy Awards for acting, but never won.

Butler, Samuel (novelist)

Samuel Butler (December 4, 1835 – June 18, 1902) was a British writer strongly influenced by his New Zealand experiences. He is best known for his utopian satire *Erewhon* and his posthumous novel *The Way of All Flesh*.

Caesar, Julius

Gaius Julius Caesar (July 13, 100 BC – March 15, 44 BC) was a Roman military and political leader and one of the most influential men in world history. He played a critical role in the transformation of the Roman Republic into the Roman Empire.

A politician of the *populares* tradition, he formed an unofficial triumvirate with Marcus Licinius Crassus and Gnaeus Pompeius Magnus which dominated Roman politics for several years, opposed in the Roman Senate by *optimates* like Marcus Porcius Cato and Marcus Calpurnius Bibulus. His conquest of Gaul extended the Roman world all the way to the Atlantic Ocean, and he also conducted the first Roman invasion of Britain in 55 BC; the collapse of the triumvirate, however, led to a stand-off with Pompey and the Senate. Leading his legions across the Rubicon, Caesar began a civil war in 49 BC from which he became the undisputed master of the Roman world.

After assuming control of government, he began extensive reforms of Roman society and government. He was proclaimed dictator for life (*dictator perpetuus*), and heavily centralized the bureaucracy of the Republic. However, a group of senators, led by Caesar's former friend Marcus Junius Brutus, assassinated the dictator on the Ides of March (March 15) in 44 BC, hoping to restore the normal running of the Republic. However, the result was another Roman civil war, which ultimately led to the establishment of a permanent autocracy by Caesar's adopted heir, Gaius Octavianus. In 42 BC, two years after his assassination, the Senate officially sanctified Caesar as one of the Roman deities.

Camden, William

William Camden (May 2, 1551 – November 9, 1623) was an English antiquarian and historian. He wrote the first topographical survey of the island of Great Britain and the first detailed historical account of the reign of Elizabeth I of England.

Canterbury, Tommy

Tommy Canterbury. No biography.

Cantor, Eddie

Eddie Cantor (January 31, 1892 – October 10, 1964) was an American comedian, singer, actor, songwriter. Known to Broadway, radio and early television audiences as **Banjo Eyes**, this "Apostle of Pep" was regarded almost as a family member by millions because his top-rated radio shows revealed intimate stories and amusing antics about his wife Ida and five children.

Capp, Al

Al Capp (September 28, 1909 – November 5, 1979) was an American cartoonist best known for the satiric comic strip, *Li'l Abner*. He also wrote the comic strips *Abbie and Slats* and *Long Sam*. He won the 1947 National Cartoonist Society Reuben Award for the comic strip *Li'l Abner*, and their 1979 Elzie Segar Award posthumously.

Capote, Truman

Truman Capote (September 30, 1924 – August 25, 1984) was an American writer whose stories, novels, plays and non-fiction are recognized literary classics, including the novella *Breakfast at Tiffany's* (1958) and *In Cold Blood* (1965), which he labeled a "non-fiction novel." At least 20 films and TV dramas have been produced from Capote novels, stories and screenplays.

Carlyle, Thomas

Thomas Carlyle (December 4, 1795 – February 5, 1881) was a Scottish essayist, and historian, whose work was hugely influential during the Victorian era. Coming from a strict Calvinist family, Carlyle was expected by his parents to become a preacher. However, while at the University of Edinburgh, he lost his Christian faith; nevertheless, Calvinist values remained with him throughout his life. This combination of a religious temperament with loss of faith in traditional Christianity made Carlyle's work appealing to many Victorians who were grappling with scientific and political changes that threatened the traditional social order.

Carson, Johnny

John William "Johnny" Carson (October 23, 1925 – January 23, 2005) was an American television host best known for his iconic status as host of *The Tonight Show Starring Johnny Carson* for thirty years.

Carter, Lillian Gordy

Bessie Lillian Gordy Carter (August 15, 1898 – October 30, 1983) was the mother of former president of the United States, Jimmy Carter. She is also known for her contribution to nursing in her home state of Georgia and as a Peace Corps volunteer in India as well as writing two books during the Carter presidency.

Catullus

Gaius Valerius Catullus (ca. 84 – 54 BC) was a Roman poet of the 1st century BC. His work remains widely studied, and continues to influence poetry and other art. Fresco from Herculaneum, presumably showing a love couple.

Chamfort, Nicolas

Nicolas Chamfort (April 6, 1741, Clermont-Ferrand, Auvergne France – April 13, 1794, Paris) was a French writer, best known for his witty epigrams and aphorisms.

Chanel, Coco

Gabrielle Bonheur "Coco" Chanel (August 19, 1883 – January 10, 1971) was a pioneering French fashion designer whose modernist philosophy, menswear-inspired fashions, and pursuit of expensive simplicity made her arguably the most important figure in the history of 20th-centruy fashion. Her influence on haute couture was such that she was the only person in the field to be named on TIME Magazine's 100 most influential people of the 20th century.

Chekhov, Anton

Anton Pavlovich Chekhov was a Russian short story writer and playwright. He was born in Taganrog, southern Russia, on 29 January 1860, and died of tuberculosis at the health spa of Badenweiler, Germany, on 15 July 1904. His playwriting career produced four classics, while his best short stories are held in high esteem by writers and critics. Chekhov practiced as a doctor throughout most of his literary career: "Medicine is my lawful wife," he once said, "and literature is my mistress".

Chekhov renounced the theatre after the disastrous reception of *The Seagull* in 1896; but the play was revived to acclaim by Constantin Stanislavski's Moscow Art Theatre, which subsequently also produced *Uncle Vanya* and premiered Chekhov's last two plays, *Three Sisters* and *The Cherry Orchard*. These four works present a special challenge to the acting ensemble as well as to audiences, because in place of conventional action Chekhov offers a "theatre of mood" and a "submerged life in the text". Not everyone appreciated that challenge: Leo Tolstoy reportedly told Chekhov, "You know, I cannot abide Shakespeare, but your plays are even worse".

Cher

Cher (born **Cherilyn Sarkisian LaPierre** on May 20, 1946) is an American singer, actress, songwriter, author and entertainer. Among her many accomplishments in music, television and film, she has won an Academy Award, a Grammy Award, an Emmy Award, a Cannes Film Award, three Golden Globe Awards, and Billboard Music Awards, among others.

Cher first rose to prominence in 1965 as one half of the pop/rock duo Sonny & Cher. She also established herself as a solo recording artist, releasing 25 albums, numerous compilations and tallying 34 *Billboard* Top 40 entries over her career, both solo and with Sonny. They include eighteen Top 10 singles and five number one singles (four solo). Cher has had 16 top ten hits in the UK between 1965 and 2003, four of which reached number one (two solo, one with Sonny, one as part of a charity single).

She became a television star in the 1970s and a film actress in the 1980s. In 1987, she won the Academy Award for Best Actress for her role in the romantic comedy *Moonstruck*.

In a career surpassing 40 years, Cher has been described as an enduring pop icon and one of the most popular female artists in music history. Since her debut in 1964, Cher has sold over 100 million records worldwide and an estimated 70 million solo singles, becoming one of the biggest-selling artists of all time.

Cherry, Don

Donald Stewart "Grapes" Cherry (born February 5, 1934 in Kingston, Ontario, Canada) is a hockey commentator for CBS Television. Cherry co-hosts the "Coach's Corner" intermission segment (with Ron MacLean) on the long running Canadian sports program *Hockey Night in Canada*. He is known for his outspoken manner, flamboyant dress, and staunch patriotism.

Besides playing and coaching hockey, he is also well-known as an author, syndicated radio commentator for The Fan Radio Network, creator of the *Rock'em Sock'em Hockey* video series, and celebrity endorser. Many consider him to be a Canadian cultural icon.

Chesterfield, Earl of

Philip Lord Chesterfield. Philip Dormer Stanhope, 4th Earl of Chesterfield PC KG (September 22, 1694 – March 24, 1773), in the County of Derby, was a title in the Peerage of England. It was created in 1616 for **Philip Stanhope**. He had already been created **Baron Stanhope**, of Shelford in the County of Nottingham, in 1616, also in the Peerage of England. Stanhope's youngest son the Hon. Alexander Stanhope was the father of James Stanhope, 1st Earl Stanhope while his half-brother Sir John Stanhope of Elvaston was the great-grandfather of William Stanhope, 1st Earl of Harrington.

Lord Chesterfield's great-great-grandson, the fourth Earl, was a politician and man of letters and notably served as Lord Lieutenant of Ireland and as Secretary of State for the Northern Department.

Chesterton, G. K.

Gilbert Keith Chesterton (May 29, 1874 – June 14, 1936) was an influential English writer of the early 20th century. His prolific and diverse output included journalism, philosophy, poetry, biography, Christian apologetics, fantasy, and detective fiction.

Chesterton has been called the "prince of paradox". He wrote in an off-hand, whimsical prose studded with startling formulations. For example: "Thieves respect property. They merely wish the property to become their property that they may more perfectly respect it." He is one of the few Christian thinkers who are equally admired and quoted by both liberal and conservative Christians, and indeed by many non-Christians. Chesterton's own theological and political views were far too nuanced to fit comfortably under the "liberal" or "conservative" banner. And in his own words he cast aspersions on the labels saying, "The whole modern world had divided itself into Conservatives and Progressives. The business of Progressives is to go on making mistakes. The business of the Conservatives is to prevent the mistakes from being corrected." He is not to be confused with his cousin A. K. Chesterton, whose political views were very different.

Child, Julia

Julia Child (August 15, 1912 – August 13, 2004) was a famous American cook, author, and television personality who introduced French cuisine and cooking techniques to the American mainstream through her many cookbooks and television programs. Her most famous works are the 1961 cookbook *Mastering the Art of French Cooking* and showcasing her sui generis television persona, the series *The French Chef*, which premiered in 1963.

Churchill, Winston

Sir Winston Leonard Spencer-Churchill, KG, OM, CH, TD, FRS, PC (Can) (30 November 1874 – 24 January 1965) was a British politician who served as Prime Minister of the United Kingdom from 1940 to 1945 and again from 1951 to 1955. A noted statesman, orator and strategist, Churchill was also an officer in the British Army. A prolific author, he won the Nobel Prize in Literature in 1953 for his historical writings.

During his army career Churchill saw combat with the Malakand Field Force on the Northwest Frontier, at the Battle of Omdurman in the Sudan and during the Second Boer War in South Africa. During this period he also gained fame, and not a small amount of notoriety, as a correspondent. At the forefront of the political scene for almost sixty years, Churchill held numerous political and cabinet positions. Before the First World War, he served as President of the Board of Trade and Home Secretary during the Liberal governments. In the First World War Churchill served in numerous positions, as First Lord of the Admiralty, Minister of Munitions, Secretary of State for War and Secretary of State for Air. He also served in the British Army on the Western Front and commanded the British Army on the Western Front and commanded the 6th Battalion of the Royal Scots Fusiliers. During the interwar years, he served as Chancellor of the Exchequer.

After the outbreak of the Second World War, Churchill was appointed First Lord of the Admiralty. Following the resignation of Neville Chamberlain on 10 May 1940, he became Prime Minister of the United Kingdom and led Britain to victory against the Axis powers. His speeches were a great inspiration to the embattled Allied forces. After losing the 1945 election, Churchill became the leader of the opposition. In 1951, Churchill again became Prime Minister before finally retiring in 1955. Upon his death, he was granted the honour, by Queen Elizabeth II of the United Kingdom, of a state funeral which saw one of the largest assemblies of statesmen in the world.

Ciardi, John

John Anthony Ciardi (June 24, 1916 – March 30, 1986) was an American poet, translator, and etymologist.

John Ciardi was primarily a poet, but he also translated Dante's *Divine Comedy*, wrote several volumes of children's poetry, pursued etymology, contributed to the *Saturday Review* as a columnist and long-time poetry editor, and directed the Bread Loaf Writers' Conference in Vermont. In 1959, Ciardi published a book on how to read, write, and teach poetry, *How Does a Poem Mean?*, which has proven to be among the most-used books of its kind. At the peak of his popularity in the early 1960s, Ciardi also had a network television program on CBS, *Accent*. For the last decade of his life, he reported on word histories on National Public Radio's *Morning Edition*, as an outgrowth of his series of books of etymologies, *A Browser's Dictionary* (1980), *A Second Browser's Dictionary* (1983) and *Good Words to You* (posthumously published in 1987). Among 20th–century American men of letters he maintained a notably high profile and level of popularity with the general public, as well as a reputation for considerable craftsmanship in his output.

Cicero

Marcus Tullius Cicero (January 3, 106 BC – December 7, 43 BC) was a Roman statesman, lawyer, political theorist, and philosopher. Cicero is widely considered one of Rome's greatest orators and prose stylists.

Cicero is generally seen as one of the most versatile minds of Roman culture and his writing the paragon of Classical Latin. He introduced the Romans to the chief schools of Greek philosophy and created a Latin philosophical vocabulary. An impressive orator and successful lawyer, Cicero likely thought his political career his most important achievement.

Clancy, Tom

Thomas Leo Clancy Jr. (born April 12, 1947), better known as Tom Clancy, is a US author of best selling political thrillers, best known for his technically detailed espionage and military science storylines set during and in the aftermath of the Cold War. His name is also a brand for similar books written by ghost writers and a series of non-fiction books on military subjects and merged biographies of key leaders. He is also part-owner of the Baltimore

Orioles, a Major League Baseball team. He officially is the Orioles' Vice Chairman of Community Projects and Public Affairs.

Colette

Colette was the pen name of the French novelist **Sidonie-Gabrielle Colette** (January 28, 1873 – August 3, 1954). She is best known, at least in the English-speaking world, for her novel *Gigi*, which provided the plot for a Lerner & Loewe musical film and stage musical.

Confucius

Confucius (*"Master Kung,"* 551 BCE – 479 BCE) was a Chinese thinker and social philosopher, whose teachings and philosophy have deeply influenced Chinese, Korean, Japanese, and Vietnamese thought and life.

His philosophy emphasized personal and governmental morality, correctness of social relationships, justice and sincerity. These values gained prominence in China over other doctrines, such as Legalism or Taoism during the Han Dynasty. Confucius' thoughts have been developed into a system of philosophy known as *Confucianism*. It was introduced to Europe by the Jesuit Matteo Ricci, who was the first to Latinise the name as "Confucius".

His teachings may be found in the *Analects of Confucius*, a collection of "brief aphoristic fragments", which was compiled many years after his death. Modern historians do not believe that any specific documents can be said to have been written by Confucius, but for nearly 2,000 years he was thought to be the editor or author of all the Five Classics such as the *Classic of Rites* (editor), and the *Spring and Autumn Annals* (author).

Cosby, Bill

William Henry "Bill" Cosby, Jr., Ed.D. (born July 12, 1937) is an American comedian, actor, television producer, activist, and luminary. A veteran stand-up performer, he got his start at various clubs,then landed a vanguard role in the 1960s action show *I Spy*. He later starred in his own series, *The Bill Cosby Show*,

in the late 1960s. He was one of the major characters on the children's television show for its first two seasons, and created the humourous educational cartoon series *Fat Albert and the Cosby Kids*, about a group of young friends growing up in the city. Cosby also acted in numerous films, although none has received the acclaim of his television work. During the 1980s, Cosby produced and starred in what is considered one of the decade's defining sitcoms, *The Cosby Show*, which aired from 1984 to 1992. The sitcom featured an upper-middle class African-American family without resorting to the kinds of stereotypes previously seen among African-Americans in prime-time television. While some argued that *The Cosby Show* ignored the issues of racial inequity still prevalent in society, many agreed that it showcased positive role models.

Coward, Noel

Sir Noel Peirce Coward (16 December 1899 – 26 March 1973) was an Academy Award winning English actor, playwright, and composer of popular music.

A student at the Italia Conti Academy stage school, Coward's first professional engagement was on 27 January 1911, in the children's play *The Goldfish*. After this appearance, he was sought after for children's roles by other professional theatres. He was cast as the Lost Boy Slightly in the 1913 production of *Peter Pan*.

Crawford, Joan

Joan Crawford (born **Lucille Fay LeSueur**; March 23, 1905 – May 10, 1977) was an Academy Award-winning American actress. The American Film Institute named Crawford among the Greatest Female Stars of All Time, ranking her at number 10.

Crisp, Quentin

Quentin Crisp (December 25, 1908 – November 21, 1999), born **Denis Charles Pratt**, was an English writer, artist's model, actor and raconteur known for his memorable and insightful witticisms. He became a gay icon in the 1970s after publication of his memoir, *The Naked Civil Servant*, brought to the attention of the general

public his defiant exhibitionism and longstanding refusal to conceal his homosexuality.

Dalí, Salvador

Salvador Domingo Felipe Jacinto Dalí Domènech, 1st Marquis of Púbol (May 11, 1904 – January 23, 1989) was a Spanish surrealist painter born in Figueres, Catalonia, Spain.

Dalí was a skilled draftsman, best known for the striking and bizarre images in his surrealist work. His painterly skills are often attributed to the influence of Renaissance masters. His best known work, *The Persistence of Memory*, was completed in 1931.

Dangerfield, Rodney

Rodney Dangerfield (November 22, 1921 – October 5, 2004) born **Jacob Cohen**, was an American comedian and actor, best known for the catchphrase "*I don't get no respect*" and his monologues on that theme.

Darrow, Clarence

Clarence Seward Darrow (April 18, 1857 Kinsman Township, Trumbull County, Ohio – March 13, 1938 Chicago) was an American lawyer and leading member of the American Civil Liberties Union, best known for defending teenage thrill killers Leopold and Loeb in their trial for murdering 14-year-old Bobby Franks (1924) and defending John T. Scopes in the so-called "Monkey" Trial (1925), in which he opposed the statesman William Jennings Bryan. He remains notable for his wit, compassion, and agnosticism that marked him as one of the most famous American lawyers and civil libertarians.

De Gaulle, Charles

Charles André Joseph Marie de Gaulle (November 22, 1890 – November 9, 1970) was a French general and statesman who led the Free French Forces during World War II and later founded the French Fifth Republic and served as its first President. In France, he is commonly referred to as *Général de Gaulle* or simply *Le Général*.

De Kooning, Willem

Willem de Kooning (April 24, 1904 – March 19, 1997) was an abstract expressionist painter, born in Rotterdam, the Netherlands.

In the post World War II era, De Kooning painted in the style that is referred to as Abstract expressionism, Action painting, and the New York School. Other painters in this category include Jackson Pollock, Franz Kline, Arshile Gorky, Mark Rothko, Hans Hofmann, Robert Motherwell, Philip Guston and Clyfford Still among others.

Dean, Dizzy

Jerome Hanna "Dizzy" Dean (January 16, 1910 – July 17, 1974) was an American pitcher in Major League Baseball, elected to the Baseball Hall of Fame. He was born in Lucas, Arkansas, and was a life-long resident of Bond, Mississippi. He was a pitcher for the St. Louis Cardinals (1930 – 1937), the Chicago Cubs (1938 – 1941), and briefly for the St. Louis Browns (1947).

Demaret, Jimmy

James Newton Demaret (May 24, 1910 – December 28, 1983) was an American professional golfer. He won 31 PGA Tour events in a long career between 1935 and 1957 and was the first three-time winner of the Masters.

Demaret was elected to the World Golf Hall of Fame in 1983. In 2000, he was ranked as the 20th greatest golfer of all time by *Golf Digest* magazine.

Dewar, Thomas Robert

Sir Thomas Robert Dewar (1864 – 1930) was a Scottish whisky distiller who, along with his brother John Dewar, built their family label, Dewar's, into an international success. They blended their whisky to make it more appealing to the international palate and Sir Thomas demonstrated particular skills in marketing, traveling the world to find new markets and promote his product, exploiting romantic images of Scotland and tartan in his advertising.

Tommy Dewar, as stated above, was an enthusiastic and gifted thinker and salesman. The founder of the "Dewarism" philosophy, he attempted to show that the way to success in life is not through an arduous or painstaking work agenda; success can be attained without compromising joy in life. This idea being the core of the philosophy, Tommy wrote smaller statements or observations that he accumulated throughout his life.

Dietrich, Marlene

Marlene Dietrich (December 27, 1901 – May 6, 1992) was a German-born American actress, singer and entertainer. She is regarded as being the first German actress to become successful in Hollywood.

Throughout her long career, starting as a cabaret singer, chorus girl and film actress in 1920s Berlin, Hollywood movie star in the 1930s, World War II frontline entertainer during the 1940s, and finally as an international stage show performer from the 1950s to the 1970s, Dietrich constantly re-invented herself and eventually became one of the entertainment icons of the 20th century. The American Film Institute ranked Dietrich No. 9 amongst the Greatest Female Stars of All Time.

Diller, Phyllis

Phyllis Diller (July 17, 1917 – August 20, 2012), a Golden Globe-nominated American comedienne, is considered one of the pioneers of female stand-up comedy. She created a stage character persona that was a wild-haired, eccentrically dressed housewife who made jokes about a fictional husband named "Fang" while smoking from a long cigarette holder. Another distinct characteristic was her cackling laugh, one of the best recognized noises in comedy. Diller is given credit for opening the locked doors for the stand-up comedy field to women such as Rita Rudner, Totie Fields, Joan Rivers, Lily Tomlin, Sandra Bernhard, Joy Behar, Rosie O'Donnell and Roseanne Barr.

Diogenes of Sinope

Diogenes "the Cynic", Greek philosopher, was born in Sinope (modern day Sinop, Turkey) about 412 BC (according to other sources 404 BC), and died in 323 BC, at Corinth. Details of his life

come in the form of anecdotes (*chreia*), especially from Diogenes Laërtius, in his book *Lives and Opinions of Eminent Philosophers*.

Diogenes of Sinope is said to have been a disciple of Antisthenes, who (according to Plato's *Phaedo*) was present at the death of Socrates. Diogenes, a beggar who made his home in the streets of Athens, made a virtue of extreme poverty. He taught contempt for human achievements; his was a relentless campaign to debunk social values and institutions.

Dirksen, Everett

Everett McKinley Dirksen (January 4, 1896 – September 7, 1969) was a Republican U.S. Congressman and Senator from Illinois. As Republican Senate leader he played a highly visible and key role in the politics of the 1960s, including helping to write and pass the Civil Rights Act of 1964. He later offered his support for the Open Housing Act of 1968, another landmark piece of Civil Rights legislation. He was one of the Senate's strongest supporters of the Vietnam War. He was a member of the Pi Kappa Alpha Fraternity.

Disraeli, Benjamin

Benjamin Disraeli, 1st Earl of Beaconsfield, KG, PC, FRS (born **Benjamin D'Israeli**; 21 December 1804 – 19 April 1881) was a British Conservative statesman and literary figure. He served in government for three decades, twice as Prime Minister – the first and thus far only person of Jewish parentage to do so (although Disraeli was baptized in the Anglican Church at 13). Disraeli's most lasting achievement was the creation of the modern Conservative Party after the Corn Laws schism of 1846.

Dostoevsky, Fyodor

Fyodor Mikhailovich Dostoevsky (November 11, 1821 – February 9, 1881) was a Russian novelist and writer of fiction whose works, including *Crime and Punishment* and *The Brothers Karamazov*, have had a profound and lasting effect on intellectual thought and world literature.

Douglas, Kirk

Kirk Douglas (born **Issur Danielovitch** on December 9, 1916) is an iconic American actor and film producer known for his cleft chin, his gravelly voice and his recurring roles as the kinds of characters Douglas himself once described as "sons of bitches". He is also father to Hollywood actor and producer Michael Douglas. He came in at #17 on AFI's list of the greatest male American screen legends of all time and is one of the two living actors (men) on the list (Sidney Poitier being the other).

Dunne, Finley Peter

Finley Peter Dunne (July 10, 1867 – April 24, 1936) was a Chicago-based U. S. author, writer and humorist. He wrote *Mr. Dooley in Peace and War* in 1898. "Mr. Dooley" became one of the first nationally syndicated newspaper features. Set in a South Side Chicago Irish pub, Mr. Dooley, the owner and bartender, would expound upon political and social issues of the day, using the thick verbiage and accent of an Irish immigrant. Dunne's sly humor and political acumen won the support of President Theodore Roosevelt, a frequent target of Mr. Dooley's barbs.

Eban, Abba

Abba Eban (born **Aubrey Solomon Meir** on 2 February 1915, died 17 November 2002) was an Israeli diplomat and politician.

Edison, Thomas

Thomas Alva Edison (February 11, 1847 – October 18, 1931) was an American inventor of Dutch origin and businessman who developed many devices that greatly influenced life around the world, including the phonograph and a long lasting light bulb. Dubbed "The Wizard of Menlo Park" by a newspaper reporter, he was one of the first inventors to apply the principles of mass production to the process of invention, and therefore is often credited with the creation of the first industrial research laboratory. Edison is considered one of the most prolific inventors in history, holding 1,093 U.S. patents in his name, as well as many patents in the United Kingdom, France and Germany.

Einstein, Albert

Albert Einstein (March 14, 1879 – April 18, 1955) was a German-born theoretical physicist. He is best known for his theory of relativity and specifically mass-energy equivalence, $E = mc^2$. Einstein received the 1921 Nobel Prize in Physics "for his services to Theoretical Physics, and especially for his discovery of the law of the photoelectric effect".

Einstein's many contributions to physics include his special theory of relativity, which reconciled mechanics with electromagnetism, and his general theory of relativity, which extended the principle of relativity to non-uniform motion, creating a new theory of gravitation. His other contributions include relativistic cosmology, capillary action, critical opalescence, classical problems of statistical mechanics and their application to quantum theory, an explanation of the Brownian movement of molecules, atomic transition probabilities, the quantum theory of a monatomic gas, thermal properties of light with low radiation density (which laid the foundation for the photon theory), a theory of radiation including stimulated emission, the conception of a unified field theory, and the geometrization of physics.

Works by Albert Einstein include more than fifty scientific papers and also non-scientific books. In 1999 Einstein was named *Time* magazine's "Person of the Century", and a poll of prominent physicists named him the greatest physicist of all time. In popular culture the name "Einstein" has become synonymous with genius.

Eisenhower, Dwight D.

Dwight David Eisenhower, born **David Dwight Eisenhower** (October 14, 1890 – March 28, 1959), nicknamed **"Ike"**, was a five-star General in the United States Army and U.S. politician, who served as the 34th President of the United States (1953 – 1961). During the Second World War, he served as Supreme Commander of the Allied forces in Europe, with responsibility for planning and supervising the successful invasion of France and Germany in 1944-45. In 1951, he became the first supreme commander of NATO.

Eisenhower was elected the 34th President as a Republican, serving for two terms. As President, he oversaw the cease-fire of the Korean War, kept up the pressure on the Soviet Union during the Cold War, made nuclear weapons a higher defense priority, launched the Space Race, enlarged the Social Security program, and began the Interstate Highway System.

Eliot, T.S.

Thomas Stearns Eliot, OM (September 26, 1888 – January 4, 1965), was a poet, dramatist and literary critic. He received the Nobel Prize in Literature in 1948. He wrote the poems *The Love Song of J. Alfred Prufrock*, *The Waste Land*, *The Hollow Men*, *Ash Wednesday*, and *Four Quartets*; the plays *Murder in the Cathedral* and *The Cocktail Party*; and the essay *Tradition and the Individual Talent*. Eliot was born an American, moved to the United Kingdom in 1914 (at the age of 25), and became a British subject in 1927 at the age of 39.

Emerson, Ralph Waldo

Ralph Waldo Emerson (May 25, 1803 – April 27, 1882) was an American essayist, poet, and leader of the Transcendentalist movement in the early 19th century.

Emerson gradually moved away from the religious and social beliefs of his contemporaries, formulating and expressing the philosophy of Transcendentalism in his 1836 essay, *Nature*. As a result of this groundbreaking work he gave a speech entitled *The American Scholar* in 1837, which is considered to be America's "Intellectual Declaration of Independence". He once said "Make the most of yourself, for that is all there is of you."

Considered one of the great orators of the time, Emerson's enthusiasm and respect for his audience enraptured crowds. His support for abolitionism late in life created controversy, and he was subject to abuse from crowds while speaking on the topic. When asked to sum up his work, he said his central doctrine was "the infinitude of the private man".

Fields, W. C.

W. C. Fields (January 29, 1880 – December 25, 1946) was an American juggler, comedian, and actor. Fields created one of the great American comic personas of the first half of the 20th century – a misanthrope who teetered on the edge of buffoonery but never quite fell in, an egotist blind to his own failings, a charming drunk; and a man who hated children, dogs and women, unless they were the wrong sort of women.

This characterization that he portrayed in films and radio was so strong that it generally identified with Fields himself. It was maintained by the then-typical movie-studio publicity departments at Fields' studios (Paramount and Universal) and further established by Robert Lewis Taylor's 1949 biography *W. C. Fields, His Follies and Fortunes*. Beginning in 1973, with the publication of Fields's letters, photos, and personal notes in grandson Ronald Fields's book *W. C. Fields by Himself*, it has been shown that Fields was married (and subsequently estranged from his wife), he financially supported their son, and he loved his grandchildren.

Fischler, Stan

Stan Fischler (born March 31, 1932 Brooklyn, New York) is a controversial hockey and New York City Subway historian, broadcaster, author and professor.

For his hockey knowledge, Fischler is known as "The Hockey Maven" in both local and national circles. Fischler is an analyst for the New Jersey Devils and New York Islanders on FSN New York and the New York Rangers on MSG. He also provides general hockey analysis on MSG and writes columns for the network's website. A consummate entertainer, Fischler is known by some to play to the cameras and has become embroiled in more than a few controversies due to a seeming desire to take contrary positions for publicity.

In addition to broadcasting, Fischler has authored or co-authored more than 90 books on hockey or the NYC subway system, frequently co-writing with his wife Shirley. His books include: *The Hockey Encyclopedia, Everybody's Hockey Book, Hockey*

Chronicle, The New NHL Encyclopedia, and most recently *MetroIce: A Century of Hockey in Greater New York,* focusing on the Rangers, Islanders and Devils franchises. His most famous subway book is *Uptown, Downtown.*

On September 18, 2007 Fischler was announced one of the four recipients of the 2007 Lester Patrick Trophy.

Flaubert, Gustave

Gustave Flaubert (December 12, 1821 – May 8, 1880) was a French writer who is counted among the greatest Western novelists. He is known especially for his first published novel, *Madame Bovary* (1857), and for his scrupulous devotion to his art and style, best exemplified by his endless search for *"le mot juste"* ("the precise word").

Florus

Florus, Roman historian, lived in the time of Trajan and Hadrian (circa 53 – 138). He compiled, chiefly from Livy, a brief sketch of the history of Rome from the foundation of the city to the closing of the temple of Janus by Augustus (25 BC). The work, which is called *Epitome de T. Livio Bellorum onmium annorum DCC Libri duo,* is written in a bombastic and rhetorical style – a panegyric of the greatness of Rome, the life of which is divided into the periods of infancy, youth and manhood. It is often wrong in geographical and chronological details. In spite of its faults, however, the book was much used in the Middle Ages and survived as a textbook into the nineteenth century.

Flynn, Errol

Errol Leslie Thomson Flynn (June 20, 1909 – October 14, 1959) was an Australian film actor, most famous for his romantic swashbuckler roles in Hollywood films and his flamboyant lifestyle.

Flynn became an overnight sensation with his first starring role in *Captain Blood* (1935). He became typecast as a swashbuckler and made a host of such films, including *The Adventures of Robin Hood* (1938), *The Dawn Patrol* (1938) with his close friend David

Niven, *Dodge City* (1939), *The Sea Hawk* (1940), and *Adventures of Don Juan* (1948).

Flynn played opposite Olivia de Havilland in eight films, including *Captain Blood*, *The Charge of the Light Brigade* (1936), *The Adventures of Robin Hood*, *Dodge City*, *Santa Fe Trail* (1940), and *They Died with Their Boots On* (1941). Film historian Rudy Behlmer asserted that during the filming of *Robin Hood*, de Havilland and Flynn were romantically involved (see the Special Edition of *Robin Hood* on DVD, 2003), but de Havilland herself has disputed this. Their relationship was, she said in an interview for Turner Classic Movies, platonic, mostly because Flynn was already married to Lili Damita. *The Adventures of Robin Hood* was Flynn's first in Technicolor.

Forbes, Malcolm

Malcolm Stevenson Forbes (August 19, 1919 – February 24, 1990) was publisher of Forbes magazine, founded by his father B.C. Forbes and today run by his son Steve Forbes.

He was a graduate of the Lawrenceville School and Princeton University, where he donated the money for Forbes College, one of the six residential colleges at the University. He received an honorary degree from Miami University in Oxford, Ohio and was initiated as an honorary member of the Alpha Chapter of Phi Kappa Tau.

After dabbling in politics, including service in the New Jersey Senate from 1951 to 1957 and candidacy for Governor of New Jersey, he committed to the magazine full time by 1957, three years after his father's death, and after the death of his brother Bruce Charles Forbes in 1964 acquired sole control of the company. The magazine grew steadily under his leadership, and he diversified into real estate sales and other ventures.

Ford, Henry

Henry Ford (July 30, 1863 – April 7, 1947) was the American founder of the Ford Motor Company and father of modern assembly lines used in mass production. His introduction of the Model T automobile revolutionized transportation and American

industry. He was a prolific inventor and was awarded 161 U.S. patents. As owner of the Ford Motor Company he became one of the richest and best-known people in the world. He is credited with "Fordism", that is, the mass production of large numbers of inexpensive automobiles using the assembly line, coupled with high wages for his workers. Ford had a global vision, with consumerism as the key to peace. Ford did not believe in accountants; he amassed one of the world's largest fortunes without ever having his company audited under his administration. Henry Ford's intense commitment to lowering costs resulted in many technical and business innovations, including a franchise system that put a dealership in every city in North America, and in major cities on six continents. Ford left most of his vast wealth to the Ford Foundation but arranged for his family to control the company permanently.

Foreman, George

George Edward Foreman (born January 10, 1949) is an American two-time World Heavyweight Boxing Champion. He is the oldest man ever to win the heavyweight title, and also has been named one of the 25 greatest fighters of all time by Ring magazine.

Nicknamed "Big George", he is now a successful businessman (well known for his Grill) and an ordained Christian minister who has his own church.

France, Anatole

Anatole France (16 April 1844 – 12 October 1924), born **François-Anatole Thibault**, was a French author. He was born in Paris, and died in Tours, Indre-et-Loire.

Anatole France became known after the publication of *The Crime of Sylvestre Bonnard* (1881). Its protagonist, skeptical old scholar Sylvester Bonnard, embodied France's own personality. The novel was praised for its elegant prose and won him a prize from the French Academy. In *La rotisserie de la Reine Pedauque* (1893) Anatole France ridiculed belief in the occult; and in *Les opinions de Jerome Coignard* (1893), France captured the atmosphere of the *fin de siècle*.

Franklin, Benjamin

Benjamin Franklin (January 17, 1706 – April 17, 1790) was one of the most important and influential Founding Fathers of the United States of America. A noted polymath, Franklin was a leading author and printer, satirist, political theorist, politician, scientist, inventor, civic activist, statesman and diplomat. As a scientist he was a major figure in the Enlightenment and the history of physics for his discoveries and theories regarding electricity. He invented the lighting rod, bifocals, the Franklin stove, a carriage odometer, and a musical instrument. He formed both the first public lending library and fire department in America.

He was an early proponent of colonial unity and as a political writer and activist he, more than anyone, invented the idea of an American nation and as a diplomat during the American Revolution, he secured the French alliance that helped to make independence possible.

Freud, Sigmund

Sigmund Freud, born **Sigismund Schlomo Freud** (May 6, 1856 – September 23, 1939), was an Austrian neurologist and psychiatrist who founded the psychoanalytic school of psychology. Freud is best known for his theories of the unconscious mind and the defense mechanism of repression. He is also renowned for his redefinition of sexual desire as the primary motivational energy of human life which is directed toward a wide variety of objects; as well as his therapeutic techniques, including his theory of transference in the therapeutic relationship and the presumed value of dreams as sources of insight into unconscious desires.

Friedman, Milton

Milton Friedman (July 31, 1912 – November 16, 2006) was an American Nobel Laureate economist and public intellectual. An advocate of economic freedom, Friedman made major contributions to the fields of macroeconomics, microeconomics, economic history and statistics. In 1976, he was awarded the Nobel Memorial Prize in Economic Sciences for his achievements in the fields of consumption analysis, monetary history and theory, and

for his demonstration of the complexity of stabilization policy.

According to *The Economist*, Friedman "was the most influential economist of the second half of the 20th century…possibly of all of it." Alan Greenspan stated "There are very few people over the generations who have ideas that are sufficiently original to materially alter the direction of civilization. Milton is one of those very few people." In his 1962 book *Capitalism and Freedom*, Friedman advocated minimizing the role of government in a free market as a means of creating political and social freedom. In his 1980 television series *Free to Choose* Friedman explained how the free market works, emphasizing that he believed that it has been shown to solve social and political problems that other systems have failed to address adequately. His books and columns for *Newsweek* were widely read and even circulated underground behind the Iron Curtain.

Frost, Robert

Robert Lee Frost (March 26, 1874 – January 29, 1963) was an American poet. His work frequently used themes from rural life in New England, using the setting to examine complex social and philosophical themes. A popular and often-quoted poet, Frost was honored frequently during his lifetime, receiving four Pulitzer Prizes.

Although he is commonly associated with New England, Robert Frost was a native of California, born in San Francisco, and lived there until he was 11 years old. His mother, Isabelle Moodie Frost, was of Scottish descent; his father, William Prescott Frost, Jr., was a descendant of colonist Nicholas Frost from Tiverton, Devon, England who had sailed to New Hampshire in 1634 on the *Wolfrana*.

Gabor, Eva

Eva Gabor (in Hungarian **Gábor Éva**) (February 11, 1919 – July 4, 1995) was a Hungarian-born actress, best known as Lisa Douglas, the wife of Eddie Albert's character Oliver Wendell Douglas, on *Green Acres*. She was the sister of Zsa Zsa Gabor and the late Magda Gabor.

Gabor, Zsa Zsa

Zsa Zsa Gábor (born February 6, 1917) is a Hungarian-born American actress and socialite. Gabor won the Miss Hungary beauty contest in 1936, but was disqualified for being underage. On a trip to Vienna in the same year she was discovered by the famous tenor Richard Tauber and was invited to sing the soubrette role in his new operetta *Der singende Traum* (*The Singing Dream*) at the Theater an der Wien, her first stage appearance.

Gabor has been married nine times. She was divorced seven times, and one marriage was annulled. Her husbands, in chronological order are:

- Burhan Belge (1937 – 1941) (divorced)
- Conrad Hilton (April 10, 1942 – 1947) (divorced)
- George Sanders (April 2, 1949 – April 2, 1954) (divorced)
- Herbert Hutner (November 5, 1962 – March 3, 1966) (divorced)
- Joshua S. Cosden, Jr. (March 9, 1966 – October 18, 1967) divorced)
- Jack Ryan (January 21, 1975 – 1976) (divorced)
- Michael O'Hara (August 27, 1976 – 1982) (divorced)
- Felipe de Alba (April 13, 1983 – April 14, 1983) (annulled)
- Frédéric Prinz von Anhalt (August 14, 1986 to present)

Zsa Zsa is the only Gábor sister to bear a child. According to Gabor's book *One Lifetime Is Not Enough* her pregnancy resulted from her being raped by Conrad Hilton. Hilton and Gabor's only child, born after their divorce, is Francesca Hilton (Gabor) born March 10, 1947. In 2005, Zsa Zsa accused her daughter, Francesca, of larceny and fraud, and filed a lawsuit against her in a California court.

Galbraith, John Kenneth

John Kenneth Galbraith (October 15, 1908 – April 29, 2006) was an influential Canadian-American economist. He was a Keynesian and an institutionalist, a leading proponent of 20th-century American liberalism and progressivism. His books on economic topics were bestsellers in the 1950s and 1960s.

Galbraith was a prolific author who produced four dozen books and over a thousand articles on various subjects. Among his most famous works was a popular trilogy on economics, *American Capitalism* (1952), *The Affluent Society* (1958), and *The New Industrial State* (1967). He taught at Harvard University for many years. Galbraith was active in politics, serving in the administrations of Franklin D. Roosevelt, Harry S. Truman, John F. Kennedy and Lyndon B. Johnson; and among other roles served as United States Ambassador to India under Kennedy.

He was one of a few two-time recipients of the Presidential Medal of Freedom. He received one from President Truman in 1946 and another from President Bill Clinton in 2000. He was also awarded the Order of Canada in 1997 and, in 2001, the Padma Vibhushan, India's second highest civilian award, for his contributions to strengthening ties between India and the United States.

Galsworthy, John

John Galsworthy OM (14 August 1867 – 31 January 1933) was an English novelist and playwright. Notable works include *The Forsyte Saga* (1906 – 1921) and its sequels, *A Modern Comedy* and *End of the Chapter*. He won the Nobel Prize in Literature in 1932.

From the Four Winds was Galsworthy's first published work in 1897, a collection of short stories. These, and several subsequent works, were published under the pen name John Sinjohn and it would not be until *The Island Pharisees* (1904) that he would begin publishing under his own name, probably owing to the death of his father. His first play, *The Silver Box* (1906) became a success, and he followed it up with *The Man of Property* (1906), the first in the Forsyte trilogy. Although he continued writing both plays and novels it was as a playwright he was mainly appreciated at the time. Along with other writers of the time such as Shaw his plays addressed the class system and social issues, two of the best known being *Strife* (1909) and *The Skin Game* (1920).

He is now far better known for his novels and particularly *The Forsyte Saga*, the first of three trilogies of novels about the eponymous family and connected lives. These books, as with many of his other works, dealt with class, and in particular upper-middle class lives. Although sympathetic to his characters he highlights their insular, snobbish and acquisitive attitudes and their suffocating moral codes. He is viewed as one of the first writers of the Edwardian era; challenging in his works some of the ideals of society depicted in the preceding literature of Victorian England. The depiction of a woman in an unhappy marriage furnishes another recurring theme in his work. The character of Irene in *The Forsyte Saga* is drawn from Ada Pearson, who became his wife, even though her previous marriage was not as miserable as Irene's.

Gauguin, Paul

Eugène Henri Paul Gauguin (7 June 1848 – 8 May 1903) was a leading Post-Impressionist painter. His bold experimentation with coloring led directly to the Synthetist style of modern art while his expression of the inherent meaning of the subjects in his paintings, under the influence of the cloisonnist style, paved the way to Primitivism and the return to the pastoral. He was also an influential exponent of wood engraving and woodcuts as art forms.

George, David Lloyd

David Lloyd-George, 1st Earl Lloyd-George of Dwyfor OM, PC (17 January 1863 – 26 March 1945) was a British statesman who was the first, and only Welsh Prime Minister that Britain has had so far. He was Prime Minister throughout the later half of World War I and the first four years of the subsequent peace.

Gleason, Jackie

Herbert John "Jackie" Gleason (February 26, 1916 – June 24, 1987) was an iconic American comedian, actor, and musician.

One of the most popular stars of early television, Gleason was respected for both comedic and dramatic roles. However, his major legacy was his brash visual and verbal comedy styling, especially as delivered by the character Ralph Kramden on the pioneering sitcom *The Honeymooners*.

Goethe, Johann Wolfgang von

Johann Wolfgan von Goethe, (28 August 1749 – 22 March 1832) was a German writer. George Eliot called him "Germany's greatest man of letters… and the last true polymath to walk the earth." Goethe's works span the fields of poetry, drama, literature, theology, humanism, and science. Goethe's *magnum opus*, lauded as one of the peaks of world literature, is the two-part dramatic poem *Faust*. Goethe's other well-known literary works include his numerous poems, the Bildungsroman *Wilhelm Meister's Apprenticeship* and the epistolary novel *The Sorrows of Young Werther*.

Goethe was one of the key figures of German literature and the movement of Weimar Classiciam in the late 18th and early 19th centuries; this movement coincides with Enlightenment, Sentimentality ("*Empfindsamkeit*"), *Sturm und Drang*, and Romanticism. The author of the scientific text *Theory of Colours*, he influenced Darwin with his focus on plant morphology.

Goldwyn, Samuel

Samuel Goldwyn (27 August 1882 – 31 January 1974) was an Academy Award and Golden Globe Award-winning producer, also a well-known Hollywood motion picture producer and founding contributor of several motion picture studios.

Gourmont, Remy de

Remy de Gourmont (April 4, 1858 – September 27, 1915) was a French Symbolist poet, novelist, and influential critic. He was widely read in his era, and an important influence on Blaise Cendrars.

Grant, Cary

Archibald Alex Leach (January 18, 1904 – November 29, 1986), better known by his stage name, **Cary Grant**, was an English-born film actor in American motion pictures. With his distinctive Mid-Atlantic accent, he was noted as perhaps the foremost exemplar of the debonair leading man, handsome, virile, charismatic and charming. He was named the second Greatest Male Star of All Time of American cinema, after Humphrey Bogart, by the American Film Institute. He was well known for starring in classic films such as *The Philadelphia Story*, *North By Northwest*, *Notorious*, *To Catch A Thief*, *Bringing Up Baby* and *The Bishop's Wife*.

Graves, Robert

Robert von Ranke Graves (24 July 1895 – 7 December 1985) was an English poet, scholar, and novelist. During his long life, he produced more than 140 works. He was the son of the Anglo-Irish writer Alfred Perceval Graves and Amalie von Ranke. The historian Leopold von Ranke was his mother's uncle. He was the brother of the author Charles Patrick Graves.

Graves considered himself a poet first and foremost. His poems, together with his innovative interpretation of the Greek Myths, his memoir of the First World War, *Good-bye to All That*, and his historical study of poetic inspiration, *The White Goddess*, have never been out of print. He earned his living from writing, particularly popular historical novels such as *I, Claudius*, *The Golden Fleece* and *Count Belisarius*. He was also a prominent translator of Classical Latin and Ancient Greek texts; his versions of *The Twelve Caesars* and *The Golden Ass* remain popular today for their clarity and entertaining style. Graves was awarded the 1934 James Tait Black Memorial Prize for both *I, Claudius* and *Claudius the God*.

Greeley, Horace

Horace Greeley (February 3, 1811 – November 29, 1872) was an American editor of a leading newspaper, a founder of the Republican party, reformer and politician. His *New York Tribune* was American's most influential newspaper from the 1840s to the 1870s and "established Greeley's reputation as the greatest editor of his day." Greeley used it to promote the Whig and Republican parties, as well as antislavery and a host of reforms. Crusading against the corruption of Ulysses S. Grant's Republican administration, he was the presidential candidate in 1872 of the new Liberal Republican Party. Despite having the additional support of the Democratic Party, he lost in a landslide.

Gretzky, Wayne

Wayne Douglas Gretzky, OC (born January 26, 1961 in Brantford, Ontario) is a retired Canadian-American professional ice hockey player who is currently part-owner and head coach of the Phoenix Coyotes.

Nicknamed "**The Great One**", Gretzky was called "the greatest player of all time" in *Total Hockey: The Official Encyclopedia of the NHL*. He is generally regarded as the best player in history and has been called "the greatest hockey player ever" by many sportswriters, players, and coaches. He set 40 regular season records, 15 playoff records, six All-Star records, won four Stanley Cups with the Edmonton Oilers, and won nine MVP awards and ten scoring titles. He is the only player ever to total over 200 points in a season (a feat that he accomplished four times in his career). In addition, he tallied over 100 points a season for 15 NHL seasons, 13 of them consecutively. He is the only player to have his number, 99, officially retired by the National Hockey League for *all teams* – no player in the NHL will ever again wear the number 99.

He retired from playing in 1999, becoming Executive Director for the Canadian national men's hockey team during the 2002 Winter Olympics. He also became part owner of the Phoenix Coyotes in 2000 and following the 2004-05 NHL lockout became their head coach.

Guinness, Alec

Sir Alec Guinness, CH, CBE (2 April 1914 – 5 August 2000) was an Academy Award and Tony Award-winning English actor. Guinness first worked writing copy for advertising before making his debut at the Albery Theatre in 1936 at the age of 22, playing the role of Osric in John Gielgud's wildly successful production of *Hamlet*.

Guinness continued playing Shakespearean roles throughout his career. In 1937 he played the role of Aumerle in *Richard II* and Lorenzo in *The Merchant of Venice* under the direction of John Gielgud. He starred in a 1938 production of *Hamlet* which won him acclaim on both sides of the Atlantic. He also appeared as Romeo in a production of *Romeo and Juliet* (1939), Andrew Aguecheck in *Twelfth Night* and as Exeter in *Henry V* in 1937, both opposite Laurence Olivier, and

Ferdinand in *The Tempest*, opposite Gielgud as Prospero.

In 1939, he adapted Charles Dickens' novel *Great Expectations* for the stage, playing the part of Herbert Pocket. The play was a success. One of its viewers was a young British film editor named David Lean, who had Guinness reprise his role in the former's 1946 film adaptation of the play.

Guinness served in the Royal Navy throughout World War II.

Guinness won particular acclaim for his work with director David Lean. After appearing in Lean's *Great Expectations* and *Oliver Twist*, he was given a starring role opposite William Holden in *Bridge on the River Kwai*. For his performance as Colonel Nicholson, the unyielding British POW leader, Guinness won an Academy Award for Best Actor.

Other famous roles of this time period included *The Swan* (1956) with Grace Kelly in her last film role, *The Horse's Mouth* (1958) in which Guinness played the part of drunken painter Gulley Jimson as well as contributing the screenplay, for which he was nominated for an Academy Award for Best Writing, Screenplay Based on Material from Another Medium, *Tunes of Glory* (1960), *Damn the Defiant!* (1962), *The Fall of the Roman Empire* (1964), *The Quiller Memorandum* (1966), *Scrooge* (1970), and the title role in *Hitler: The Last Ten Days* (1973) (which he considered his best film performance).

Guinness' role as Obi-Wan Kenobi in the original *Star Wars* trilogy, beginning in 1977, brought him worldwide recognition by a new generation. Guinness agreed to take the part on the condition that he would not have to do publicity to promote the film. He was also one of the few cast members who believed that the film would be a box office hit and negotiated a deal for two percent of the gross, which made him very wealthy in later life.

Hamilton, Alexander

Alexander Hamilton (January 11, 1755 – July 12, 1804) was an Army officer, lawyer, Founding Father, American politician, leading statesman, financier and political theorist. One of America's first constitutional lawyers, he was a leader in calling the Philadelphia Convention in 1787; he was one of the two

chief authors of the anonymous *Federalist Papers*, the most cited contemporary interpretation of intent for the United States Constitution.

During the Revolutionary War, Hamilton served as an artillery captain, was an aide-de-camp to General George Washington, and led three battalions at the Battle of Yorktown. Under President Washington, Hamilton became the first Secretary of the Treasury. As Secretary of the Treasury and confidant of Washington, Hamilton had wide-reaching influence over the direction of policy during the formative years of the government. Hamilton believed in the importance of a strong central government, and convinced Congress to use an elastic interpretation of the Constitution to pass far-reaching laws. They included: the funding of the national debt; federal assumption of the state debts; creation of a national bank; and a system of taxes through a tariff on imports and a tax on whiskey that would help pay for it. He admired the success of the British system – particularly its strong financial and trade networks – and opposed what he saw as the excesses of the French Revolution.

Heine, Heinrich

Christian Johann Heinrich Heine (December 13, 1797 – February 17, 1856) was a journalist, essayist, and one of the most significant German romantic poets. He is remembered chiefly for selections of his lyric poetry, many of which were set to music in the form of *lieder* (art songs) by German composers.

Heinlein, Robert A.

Robert Anson Heinlein (July 7, 1907 – May 8, 1988) was one of the most popular, influential, and controversial authors of "hard science fiction". He set a high standard for science and engineering plausibility and helped to raise the genre's standards of literary quality. He was the first writer to break into mainstream, general magazines such as *The Saturday Evening Post*, in the late 1940s, with unvarnished science fiction. He was among the first authors of best selling, novel-length science fiction in the modern, mass-market era. For many years, Heinlein, Isaac Asimov, and Arthur C. Clarke were known as the "Big Three" of science fiction.

Hemingway, Ernest

Ernest Miller Hemingway (July 21, 1899 – July 2, 1961) was an American novelist, short story writer, and journalist . Nicknaming himself "*Papa*" while still in his 20s, he was part of the 1920s expatriate community in Paris known as "the Lost Generation", as described in his memoir *A Moveable Feast*. Hemingway received the Pulitzer Prize in 1953 for *The Old Man and the Sea*. He received the Nobel Prize in Literature in 1954. During his later life, Hemingway suffered from increasing physical and mental problems. In July 1961, after being released from a mental hospital where he'd been treated for severe depression, he committed suicide at his home in Ketchum, Idaho with a shotgun.

Hepburn, Katharine

Katharine Houghton Hepburn (May 12, 1907 – June 29, 2003) was an iconic American actress of film, television and stage.

A screen legend, Hepburn holds the record for the most Best Actress Oscar wins with four, from twelve nominations (Meryl Streep currently holds the record for most overall acting nominations with eighteen). Hepburn won an Emmy Award in 1975 for her lead role in *Love Among the Ruins* opposite her friend Laurence Olivier, and was nominated for four other Emmys and two Tony Awards during the course of her more than 70-year acting career. In 1999, the American Film Institute ranked Hepburn as the top female star of all time.

Herford, Oliver

Oliver Herford (1863 – 1935) was a British born American writer, artist and illustrator who has been called "The American Oscar Wilde". As a frequent contributor to *The Mentor*, *Life*, and *Ladies' Home Journal*, he sometimes signed his artwork as "O'Herford". In 1906 he wrote and illustrated the *Little Book of Bores*. He also wrote short poems like "The Chimpanzee" and "The Hen", as well as writing and illustrating "The Rubaiyat of a Persian Kitten" (1904), "Cynic's Calendar" (1917) and "Excuse It Please" (1930). His sister Beatrice Herford was also a humorist.

Herold, Don

Don Herold (July 9, 1889 – June 1, 1966) was an American humorist, writer, illustrator, and cartoonist who wrote and illustrated many books and was a contributor to national magazines.

Hitchcock, Alfred

Sir Alfred Joseph Hitchcock, KBE (August 13, 1899 – April 29, 1980) was an iconic and highly influential English-born American film director and producer who pioneered many techniques in the suspense and thriller genres. He directed more than fifty feature films in a career spanning six decades, from the silent film era, through the invention of talkies, to the color era. Hitchcock was among the most consistently successful and publicly recognizable world directors during his lifetime, and remains one of the best known and most popular of all time.

Famous for his expert and largely unrivalled control of pace and suspense, Hitchcock's films draw heavily on both fear and fantasy, and are known for their droll humour and witticisms. They often portray innocent people caught up in circumstances beyond their control or understanding.

Hitler, Adolf

Adolf Hitler (April 20, 1889 – April 30, 1945) was a German politician, who became the Leader of the National Socialist German Workers Party and was appointed as the Chancellor of Germany in 1933. After the death of President Paul Von Hindenburg in 1934, Hitler declared himself Führer, combining the offices of President and Chancellor into one using the power vested in him by the Enabling Act, and remained in the position of Führer until his eventual suicide in 1945.

The Nazi Party gained power during Germany's period of crisis after World War I, exploiting effective propaganda and Hitler's charismatic oratory to gain popularity. The Party emphasized nationalism and anti-semitism as its primary political expressions, eventually resorting to murdering its opponents to ensure success.

After the restructuring of the state economy and the rearmament of the Wehrmacht, a dictatorship (commonly characterized as either totalitarian or fascist) was established by Hitler, who then pursued an aggressive foreign policy, with the goal of seizing *Lebensraum*. This resulted in the German Invasion of Poland in 1939, drawing the British and French Empires into World War II.

The Wehrmacht enjoyed great success in the early stages of the war, and the Axis Powers managed to occupy most of Mainland Europe and parts of Asia and Africa at the height of their power. Eventually however, the occupation was rolled back by the combined efforts of the Allies after a long struggle, and the Wehrmacht was ultimately defeated. By 1945, both Hitler's policy and the Nazi Party lay in ruins; his bid for territorial conquest and racial subjugation had caused the deaths of tens of millions of people, including the deliberate genocide of an estimated six million Jews in what is now known as the Holocaust.

During the final days of the war in 1945, as the German capital of Berlin was being invaded and destroyed by the Red Army of the Soviet Union, Hitler married Eva Braun and less than 24 hours later, the two committed suicide in the Führerbunker.

Holmes, Jr., Oliver Wendell

Oliver Wendell Holmes, Jr. (March 8, 1841 – March 6, 1935) was an American jurist who served on the Supreme Court of the United States from 1902 to 1932. Noted for his long service, his concise and pithy opinions, and his deference to the decisions of elected legislatures, he is one of the most widely cited United States Supreme Court justices in history, particularly for his "clear and present danger" majority opinion in the 1919 case of *Schenck v. United States*, as well as one of the most influential American common-law judges.

Hoover, Herbert

Herbert Clark Hoover (August 10, 1874 – October 20, 1964), the thirty-first President of the United States (1929 – 1933), was a mining engineer and humanitarian administrator. As the United States Secretary of Commerce in the 1920s under Presidents Warren Harding and Calvin Coolidge, he promoted economic modernization. In the presidential election of 1928 Hoover easily won the Republican nomination. The nation was prosperous and optimistic, leading to a landslide for Hoover over the Democrat Al Smith, a Catholic whose religion was distrusted by many. Hoover deeply believed in the Efficiency Movement (a major component of the Progressive Era), arguing that there were technical solutions to all social and economic problems. That position was challenged by the Great Depression, which began in 1929, the first year of his presidency. He tried to combat the Depression with volunteer efforts and government action, none of which produced economic recovery during his term. The consensus among historians is that Hoover's defeat in the 1932 election was caused primarily by failure to end the downward spiral into deep Depression, compounded by popular opposition to Prohibition. Other electoral liabilities were Hoover's lack of charisma in relating to voters, and his poor skills in working with politicians.

Hope, Bob

Bob Hope KBE (May 29, 1903 – July 27, 2003) was an English-born entertainer who appeared in vaudeville, on Broadway, in radio, television, movies, and on numerous USO tours for U.S. military personnel.

Born Leslie Townes Hope in Eltham, London, England, Hope was the fifth of seven sons. His English father, William Henry Hope, was a stonemason from Weston-super-Mare and his Welsh mother, Avis Townes, was a light opera singer but later had to find work as a cleaning woman. The family lived in Weston-super-Mare, then Whitehall and St. George in Bristol, before moving to Cleveland, Ohio in 1908. The family traveled to the United States as passengers on board the SS Philadelphia. They were inspected at Ellis Island on 30 March 1908. Hope became a U.S. citizen in 1920 at the age of seventeen.

Hopper, Edward

Edward Hopper (July 12, 1882 – May 15, 1967) was an American painter and printmaker. While most popularly known for his oil paintings, he was equally proficient was a watercolorist and printmaker in etching.

Horne, Lena

Lena Mary Calhoun Horne (June 30, 1917 in Bedford-Stuyvesant, Brooklyn, New York – May 9, 2010 in New York) was a popular singer of African-American descent. She recorded and performed extensively with jazz musicians (notably Artie Shaw, Teddy Wilson), Billy Strayhorn, and Duke Ellington. She might be best-known for her version of the song "Stormy Weather", which was a hit in the 1940s.

Hubbard, Kin

Frank McKinney Hubbard (September 1, 1868 in Bellefontaine, Ohio – December 26, 1930 in Indianapolis, Indiana) was an American cartoonist, humorist, and journalist better known by his pen name **"Kin" Hubbard**.

He was creator of the cartoon "Abe Martin of Brown County" which ran in U.S. newspapers from 1904 until his death in 1930, and was the originator of many political quips that remain in use. North American humorist Will Rogers declared Kin to be "America's greatest humorist".

Hughes, Rupert

Rupert Hughes (1872 – 1956) was a historian, novelist, film director, and composer based in Hollywood. Hughes was born in Lancaster, Missouri. His parents were Felix Turner Hughes and Jean Amelia Summerlin, who were married in 1865. His brother Howard R. Hughes, Sr., co-founded the Hughes Tool Company. He was the uncle of Howard Hughes. His three volume scholarly biography of George Washington broke new ground in demythologizing the general and was well received by historians.

Hughes, active in state politics, was one of the founders of the California State Guard in 1940.

Hugo, Victor

Victor-Marie Hugo (February 26, 1802 – May 22, 1885) was a French poet, playwright, novelist, essayist, visual artist, statesman, human rights campaigner, and perhaps the most influential exponent of the Romantic movement in France.

In France, Hugo's literary reputation rests primarily on his poetic and dramatic output and only secondarily on his novels. Among many volumes of poetry, *Les Contemplations* and *La Légende des siècles* stand particularly high in critical esteem, and Hugo is sometimes identified as the greatest French poet. In the English-speaking world his best-known works are often the novels *Les Misérables* and *Notre-Dame de Paris* (sometimes translated into English as *The Hunchback of Notre-Dame*).

Hume, David

David Hume (April 26, 1711 – August 25, 1776) was an 18th-century Scottish philosopher, economist, and historian, considered among the most important figures in the history of Western philosophy and the Scottish Enlightenment. He first gained recognition and respect as a historian, but interest in Hume's work in academia has in recent years centered on his philosophical writing. His *History of England* was the standard work on English history for sixty or seventy years until Macaulay's.

Huxley, Aldous

Aldous Leonard Huxley (July 26, 1894 – November 22, 1963) was an English writer and one of the most prominent members of the famous Huxley family. He spent the latter part of his life in the United States, living in Los Angeles from 1937 until his death in 1963. Best known for his novels and wide-ranging output of essays, he also published short stories, poetry, travel writing, and film stories and scripts. Through his novels and essays Huxley functioned as an examiner and sometimes critic of social mores, norms and ideals. Huxley was a humanist but was also interested towards the end of his life in spiritual subjects such as parapsychology and philosophical mysticism. By the end of his life Huxley was considered, in some academic circles, a leader of modern thought and an intellectual of the highest rank.

Huxley, Thomas Henry

Thomas Henry Huxley PC, FRS (4 May 1825 Ealing – 29 June 1895 Eastbourne, Sussex) was an English biologist, known as "Dawin's Bulldog" for his advocacy of Charles Darwin's theory of evolution.

Ingersoll, Robert G.

Colonel **Robert Green Ingersoll** (August 11, 1833 – July 21, 1899) was a Civil War veteran, American political leader, and orator during the Golden Age of Free Thought, noted for his broad range of culture and his defense of agnosticism.

Jackson, Stonewall

Thomas Jonathan "Stonewall" Jackson (January 21, 1824 – May 10, 1863) was a Confederate general during the American Civil War, and probably the most revered Confederate commander after General Robert E. Lee. He is most famous for his audacious Valley Campaign of 1862 and as a corps commander in the Army of Northern Virginia under Robert E. Lee. A Confederate picket accidentally shot him at the Battle of Chancellorsville on May 2nd, 1863, which the general survived, albeit with the loss of an arm to amputation. However, he died of complications of pneumonia eight days later, on May 10th, 1863.

Military historians consider Jackson to be one of the most gifted tactical commanders in United States history. His Valley Campaign and his envelopment of the Union Army right wing at Chancellorsville are studied worldwide even today as examples of innovative and bold leadership. He excelled as well at the First Battle of Bull Run (where he received his famous nickname "Stonewall"), Second Bull Run, Antietam, and Fredericksburg. Jackson was not universally successful as a commander, however, as displayed by his weak and confused efforts during the Seven

Days Battles around Richmond in 1862. His death was a severe setback for the Confederacy, affecting not only its military prospects, but the morale of its army and the general public; as Jackson lay dying, General Robert E. Lee sent a message to Jackson through Chaplain Lacy, saying "Give General Jackson my affectionate regards, and say to him: he has lost his left arm but I my right."

James, William

William James (January 11, 1842 – August 26, 1910) was a pioneering American psychologist and philosopher. He wrote influential books on the young science of psychology, educational psychology, psychology of religious experience and mysticism, and the philosophy of pragmatism. He was the brother of novelist Henry James and of diarist Alice James.

Jefferson, Thomas

Thomas Jefferson (April 13, 1743 – July 4, 1826) was the third President of the United States (1801 – 1809), the principal author of the Declaration of Independence (1776), and one of the most influential Founding Fathers for his promotion of the ideals of Republicanism in the United States. Major events during his presidency include the Louisiana Purchase (1803) and the Lewis and Clark Expedition (1804 – 1806).

As a political philosopher, Jefferson was a man of the Enlightenment and knew many intellectual leaders in Britain and France. He idealized the independent yeoman farmer as exemplar of republican virtues, distrusted cities and financiers, and favored states' rights and a strictly limited federal government. Jefferson supported the separation of church and state and was the author of the Virginia Statute for Religious Freedom (1779, 1786). He was the eponym of Jeffersonian democracy and the co-founder and leader of the Democratic-Republican Party, which dominated American politics for a quarter-century and was the precursor of the modern-day Democratic Party. Jefferson served as the wartime Governor of Virginia (1779 – 1781), first United States Secretary of State (1789 – 1793) and second Vice President (1797 – 1801).

Jesus

Jesus (7- 2 BC/BCE to 26 – 36 AD/CE), also known as **Jesus of Nazareth**, was a 1st century Jewish leader who is the central figure of Christianity, and is also an important figure in several other religions. He is also called **Jesus Christ**, where "Christ" is a title derived from the Greek (*Christós*), meaning the "Anointed One", which corresponds to the Hebrew-derived "Messiah". The name "Jesus" is an Anglicization of the Greek (*Iēsous*), itself a Hellenization of the Hebrew (*Yehoshua*) or Hebrew-Aramaic (*Yeshua*), meaning "YHWH rescues".

The main sources of information regarding Jesus' life and teachings are the four canonical Gospels of the New Testament: Matthew, Mark, Luke, and John. Most scholars in the fields of history and biblical studies agree that Jesus was a Galilean Jew, was regarded as a teacher and healer, was baptized by John the Baptist, and was crucified in Jerusalem on orders of the Roman Governor Pontius Pilate under the accusation of sedition against the Roman Empire. Few critical scholars believe that all ancient texts on Jesus' life are either completely accurate or completely inaccurate.

Johnson, Lyndon B.

Lyndon Baines Johnson (August 27, 1908 – January 22, 1973), often referred to as **LBJ**, was the thirty-sixth President of the United States (1963 – 1969). Johnson served a long career in the U.S. Congress, and in 1960 was selected by then-Presidential candidate John F. Kennedy to be his running-mate. Johnson became the thirty-seventh Vice President, and in 1963, he succeeded to the presidency following Kennedy's assassination. He was a major leader of the Democratic Party and as President was responsible for designing the Great Society, comprising liberal legislation including civil rights laws. Medicare (health care for the elderly), Medicaid (health care for the poor), aid to education, and a "War on Poverty". Simultaneously, he escalated the American involvement in the Vietnam War, from 16,000 American soldiers in 1963 to 550,000 in early 1968.

He was elected President in his own right in a landslide victory in 1964, but his popularity steadily declined after 1966 and his reelection bid in 1968 collapsed as a result of turmoil in his party. He withdrew from the race to concentrate on peacemaking. Johnson was renowned for his domineering (or dominating) personality and the "Johnson treatment", his arm-twisting of powerful politicians.

Johnson suffered a massive heart attack in 1973, the third in his lifetime. He died on January 22, 1973.

Johnson, Samuel

Samuel Johnson LL.D. MA (September 18, 1709 – 13 December 1784), often referred to simply as **Dr Johnson**, is one of England's best known literary figures: an essayist, biographer, lexicographer and a critic of English Literature. He was also a great wit and prose stylist, well known for his *aphorisms*. Dr Johnson is the most quoted English writer after Shakespeare and has been described as one of the outstanding figures of 18th-century England.

Joubert, Joseph

Joseph Joubert (born May 7, 1754 in Montignac, Périgord and died May 4, 1824 in Villeneuve-sur-Yonne) was a French moralist and essayist, remembered today largely for his *Pensées* published posthumously.

From age 14 Joubert attended a religious college in Toulouse, where he later taught until 1776. In 1778 he went to Paris where he met D'Alembert and Diderot, among others, and later became friends with young writer and diplomat Chateaubriand.

He alternated between living in Paris with his friends and life in the privacy of the countryside in Villeneuve-sur-Yonne. He was appointed inspector-general of the University under Napoleon.

Somewhat of the Epicurean school of philosophy, Joubert enjoyed even his own suffering as he believed sickness gave subtlety to the soul.

Joubert's works have been translated into numerous languages, into English by Paul Auster, among others.

Joyce, James

James Augustine Aloysius Joyce (2 February 1882 – 13 January 1941) was an Irish expatriate writer, widely considered to be one of the most influential writers of the 20th century. He is best known for his landmark novel *Ulysses* (1922) and its highly controversial successor *Finnegans Wake* (1939), as well as the short story collection *Dubliners* (1914) and the semi-autobiographical novel *A Portrait of the Artist as a Young Man* (1916).

Kant, Immanuel

Immanuel Kant (22 April 1724 – 12 February 1804) was an 18th-century German philosopher from the Prussian city of Königsberg (now Kaliningrad, Russia). He is regarded as one of the most influential thinkers of modern Europe and of the late Enlightenment.

Kaufman, George S.

George Kaufman (November 16, 1889 – June 2, 1961) was an American playwright, theatre director and producer, humorist, and drama critic.

His Broadway debut was in 1918 with the now-forgotten *Someone in the House*, written with Larry Evans and W. C. Percival. This play was panned, and it had the further handicap of opening on Broadway during a flu epidemic, when theatre attendance in New York City diminished drastically because the public were warned to avoid crowds. Kaufman sardonically advised his play's producers to print advertisements with this message: "Avoid crowds: see *Someone in the House*."

It would be quite a long time before Kaufman had another flop. In every Broadway season from 1921 through 1958, there was a play written or directed by Kaufman. Since Kaufman's death in 1961, every decade has featured at least a couple of revivals of his work. There have also been productions based on Kaufman properties, such as the 1981 musical version of *Merrily We Roll Along*, adapted by George Furth and Stephen Sondheim.

Kaufman was known as "The Great Collaborator" because he

wrote very few plays alone. His most successful solo script was *The Butter and Egg Man* in 1925. With others, Kaufman was prolific: with Marc Connelly he wrote *Merton of the Movies*, *Dulcy*, and *Beggar on Horseback*; with Ring Lardner he wrote *June Moon*.

Keillor, Garrison

Garrison Keillor (born **Gary Edward Keillor** on August 7, 1942 in Anoka, Minnesota) is an American author, storyteller, humorist, columnist, musician, satirist, and radio personality.

He is best known as host of the Minnesota Public Radio show *A Prairie Home Companion* (also known as *Garrison Keillor's Radio Show* on Britain's BBC 7, as well as on Australia's ABC and in Ireland).

Kennedy, Florynce

Florynce Kennedy (February 11, 1916 – December 22, 2000) was a lawyer, activist, civil rights advocate, and feminist.

Her activism is divided into two parts: feminism and civil rights. In feminism, she often traveled with writer Gloria Steinem, talking to women in a speaking tour. If a man asked the pair if they were lesbians – a stereotype of feminists at the time – Flo would famously answer, "Are you my alternative?" In 1971 she founded the Feminist Party, which nominated Shirley Chisholm for president. She also helped found the Women's Political Caucus and the National Organization for Women.

She is also known for her pro-choice activism on abortion, writing a book called *Abortion Rap*, and stating that "If men could get pregnant, abortion would be a sacrament."

Kennedy, John F.

John Fitzgerald Kennedy (May 29, 1917 – November 22, 1963) was the thirty-fifth President of the United States, serving from 1961 until his assassination in 1963.

After Kennedy's military service as commander of the USS *PT-109* during World War II in the South Pacific, his aspirations turned political. Kennedy represented the state of Massachusetts in the U.S. House of Representatives from 1947 to 1953 as a Democrat, and in the U.S. Senate from 1953 until 1961. Kennedy defeated former Vice President and Republican candidate Richard Nixon in the 1960 U.S. presidential election, one of the closest in American history. To date, he is the only practicing Roman Catholic to be elected President and the only President to have won a Pulitzer Prize. Events during his administration include the Bay of Pigs Invasion, the Cuban Missile Crisis, the building of the Berlin Wall, the Space Race, the American Civil Rights Movement and early events of the Vietnam War.

Kennedy was assassinated on November 22, 1963, in Dallas, Texas. Lee Harvey Oswald was charged with the crime, but was murdered two days later by Jack Ruby before he could be put on trial. The Warren Commission concluded that Oswald had acted alone in killing the president; however, the House Select Committee on Assassinations declared in 1979 that there was more likely a conspiracy that included Oswald. The entire subject remains controversial, with multiple theories about the assassination still being debated. The event proved to be a poignant moment in U.S. history because of its impact on the nation and the ensuing political repercussions. Many regard President Kennedy as an icon of American hopes and aspirations; he continues to rank highly in public opinion ratings of former U.S. presidents.

Kennedy, Rose Fitzgerald

Rose Fitzgerald Kennedy (July 22, 1890 – January 22, 1995) was the wife of Joseph Kennedy and the mother of President John Fitzgerald Kennedy.

Keynes, John Maynard

John Maynard Keynes, 1st Baron Keynes, CB (5 June 1883 – 21 April 1946) was a British economist whose ideas, called Keynesian economics, had a major impact on modern economic and political theory as well as on many governments' fiscal policies. He advocated interventionist government policy, by which the government would use fiscal and monetary measures to mitigate the adverse effects of economic recessions, depressions and booms. He is one of the fathers of modern theoretical macroeconomics.

Khayyám, Omar

Ghiyās od īn Abul Fatah Omār ibn Ibrāhīm Khayyām Nishābūrī or **Omar Khayyam** (Nishapur, Persia, May 18, 1048 – December 4, 1131) was a Persian poet, mathematician, philosopher and astronomer who lived in Persia. His name is also given as **Omar al-Khayyami**.

He is best known for his poetry, and outside Iran, for the quatrains (*rubaiyaas*) in *Rubaiyat of Omar Khayyam*, popularized through Edward Fitzgerald's re-created translation. His substantial mathematical contributions include his *Treatise on Demonstration of Problems of Algebra*, which gives a geometric method for solving cubic equations by intersecting a hyperbola with a circle. He also contributed to calendar reform and may have proposed a heliocentric theory well before Copernicus.

Khrushchev, Nikita

Nikita Sergeyevich Khrushchev (April 17, 1894 – September 11, 1971) served as First Secretary of the Communist Party of the Soviet Union from 1953 to 1964, following the death of Joseph Stalin, and Chairman of the Council of Ministers from 1958 to 1964. Khrushchev's party colleagues removed him from power in 1964, replacing him with Leonid Brezhnev. He spent the last seven years of his life under the close supervision of the KGB.

Kierkegaard, Soren

Soren Aabye Kierkegaard (5 May 1813 – 11 November 1855) was a prolific 19th century Danish philosopher and theologian. Kierkegaard strongly criticized both the Hegelianism of his time, and what he saw as the empty formalities of the Danish church. Much of his work deals with religious problems such as the nature of faith, the institution of the Christian Church, Christian ethics and theology, and the emotions and feelings of individuals when faced with life choices. His early work was written under various pseudonyms who present their own distinctive viewpoints in a complex dialogue. Kierkegaard left the task of discovering the meaning of the works to the reader, because "the task must be made difficult, for only the difficult inspires the noble-hearted". Subsequently, many have interpreted Kierkegaard as an existentialist, neo-orthodoxist, postmodernist, humanist, individualist, etc. Crossing the boundaries of philosophy, theology, psychology, and literature, Kierkegaard came to be regarded as a highly significant and influential figure in contemporary thought.

King, Frank

Frank King (April 9, 1883 – June 24, 1969) was an American cartoonist most famous for the comic strip *Gasoline Alley*.

Born in Cashton, Wisconsin, King grew up in Tomah, Wisconsin and attended the Chicago Academy of Fine Arts.

He broke into professional cartoonist at the *Minneapolis Times* in 1901 and moved through the decade to *Chicago's American*, the *Chicago Examiner*, and finally, in 1910, the *Chicago Tribune*.

King created several recurring strips, including *Tough Teddy*, *The Boy Animal Trainer*, *Here Comes Motorcycle Mike*, *Hi Hopper*, and, his first successful full-page comic, *Bobby Make-Believe* in 1915. King produced a black and white cartoon page, since 1914 named *The Rectangle*, featuring a variety of cartoons and serial features.

Gasoline Alley emerged from a corner of this page, first titled *Sunday morning in Gasoline Alley*, in 1918. A great success, the strip would become the first to portray the aging process of characters, and be regarded as the comics' first soap opera. Although King retired from drawing *Gasoline Alley* in 1951, the strip is still running as of 2014.

King, Jr., Martin Luther

Martin Luther King, Jr. (January 15, 1929 – April 4, 1968) was one of the main leaders of the American civil rights movement. A Baptist minister by training, King became a civil rights activist early in his career, leading the Montgomery Bus Boycott and helping to found the Southern Christian Leadership Conference. His efforts led to the 1963 March on Washington, where King delivered his "I Have a Dream" speech, raising public consciousness of the civil rights movement and establishing King as one of the greatest orators in American history. In 1964, King

became the youngest person to receive the Nobel Peace Prize for his efforts to end segregation and racial discrimination through civil disobedience and other non-violent means.

King was assassinated on April 4, 1968, in Memphis, Tennessee. He was posthumously awarded the Presidential Medal of Freedom by President Jimmy Carter in 1977. Martin Luther King Day was established as a national holiday in the United States in 1986. In 2004, King was posthumously awarded a Congressional Gold Medal.

Kipling, Rudyard

Joseph Rudyard Kipling (December 30, 1865 – January 18, 1936) was an English author and poet, born in Bombay, India, and best known for his works *The Jungle Book* (1894), *The Second Jungle Book* (1895), *Just So Stories* (1902), and *Puck of Pook's Hill* (1906); his novel, *Kim* (1901); his poems, including *Mandalay* (1890), *Gunga Din* (1890), and "If –" (1910); and his many short stories, including "The Man Who Would Be King" (1888) and the collections *Life's Handicap* (1891), *The Day's Work* (1898), and *Plain Tales from the Hills* (1888). He is regarded as a major "innovator" in the art of the short story; his children's books are enduring classics of children's literature; and his best work speaks to a versatile and luminous narrative gift.

Kissinger, Henry

Henry Alfred Kissinger (born **Heinz Alfred Kissinger** on May 27, 1923) is a German-born American politician, and 1973 Nobel Peace Prize laureate. He served as National Security Advisor and later concurrently as Secretary of State in the Richard Nixon administration. Kissinger emerged unscathed from the Watergate scandal and maintained his powerful position when Gerald Ford became President.

A proponent of *Realpolitik*, Kissinger played a dominant role in United States foreign policy between 1969 and 1977. During this period, he pioneered the policy of *détente* to publicly show the U.S. as showing kindness to Soviets while it secretly warred with other countries.

During his time in the Nixon and Ford administrations he cut a flamboyant figure, appearing at social occasions with many celebrities. His foreign policy record made him enemies among the anti-war left and among the anti-Communist right alike.

Kraus, Karl

Karl Kraus (April 28, 1874 – June 12, 1936) was an eminent Austrian writer and journalist, known as a satirist, essayist, aphorist, playwright and poet. He is generally considered one of the foremost German-language satirists of the 20th century, especially known for his witty criticism of the press, German culture, and German and Austrian politics.

Lauder, Estée

Estée Lauder (July 1, 1908 – April 24, 2004) was the co-founder, with her husband Joseph Lauder, of Estée Lauder Companies, a pioneering cosmetics company. She was born **Josephine Esther Mentzer** in Corona, Queens, New York, the daughter of Hungarian Jewish immigrants. She was the only woman on *Time* magazine's 1998 list of the 20 most influential business geniuses of the 20th century. She was the recipient of the Presidential Medal of Freedom.

She married Joseph Lauter in 1930. They had two sons. Estée divorced Joseph in 1939, and re-married him in 1942. The couple remained married thereafter until his death in 1982. The Lauter family changed their surname to "Lauder" in the late 1930s. Her older son, Leonard Lauder, was chief executive of Estée Lauder and is now chairman of the board. Her younger son, Ronald Lauder, is a prominent philanthropist, a Republican political appointee in the Reagan administration, and developer of property in Berlin, among other endeavors.

Lebowitz, Fran

Frances Ann "Fran" Lebowitz (b. October 27, 1950) is an American author. Born in Morristown, New Jersey, Lebowitz is best known for her sardonic social commentary on American life through her New York sensibilities. Some reviewers have called her a modern day Dorothy Parker.

After being expelled from high school and receiving a GED, Lebowitz worked many odd jobs before being hired by Andy Warhol as a columnist for *Interview*. This was followed by a stint at *Mademoiselle*. Her first book was a collection of essays titled *Metropolitan Life*, released in 1978, followed by *Social Studies* in 1981, both of which are collected (with a new introductory essay) in *The Fran Lebowitz Reader*.

For more than twenty years she has been famous in part for not writing *Exterior Signs of Wealth*, a long-overdue novel purportedly about rich people who want to be artists, and artists who want to be rich. Recently she has made recurring appearances as Judge Janice Goldberg on the television drama *Law & Order*.

Lee, Gypsy Rose

Gypsy Rose Lee (also known as **Rose Louise Hovick** and **Louise Hovick**) (February 9, 1911/1914 – April 26, 1970) was an American actress, burlesque entertainer, and writer whose 1957 memoir, which included a scathing portrait of her domineering mother, was made into the stage musical and film *Gypsy*.

Leno, Jay

James Douglas Muir "Jay" Leno (April 28, 1950) is an Emmy Award-winning American comedian and television host, who succeeded Johnny Carson as host of *The Tonight Show* in 1992, and hosted his last episode of the show on February 6, 2014.

Levant, Oscar

Oscar Levant (December 27, 1906 – August 14, 1972) was an American pianist, composer, author, comedian, and actor. He was more famous for his mordant character and witticisms, on the radio and in movies and television, than for his music.

Levenson, Sam

Sam Levenson (December 28, 1911 – August 27, 1980) was an American humorist, writer, television host and journalist.

Sam Levenson was a Spanish teacher before writing the bestselling *Sex and the Single Child* (1969), *One Era And Out The Other* (1973), *You Can Say That Again, Sam!* (1975), and *Everything But Money* (1966). He hosted the game show *Two for the Money* in 1956 (taking over for Herb Shriner) and the *Sam Levenson Show* from 1959 to 1964. Over a span of more than a decade, he appeared on *Toast of the Town* aka *The Ed Sullivan Show* 21 times, in addition to frequently serving as a substitute host on CBS's *Arthur Godfrey Time*. He was a guest host on *The Price is Right* and was a panelist on many other television programs such as *Password* and *What's My Line*. Levenson also had a cameo in the film *A Face in the Crowd*. He also appeared multiple times on *The Tonight Show with Johnny Carson* throughout the 1970s. Levenson also wrote the well-known poem "Time Tested Beauty Tips" for his grandchild, which has become falsely attributed to Audrey Hepburn.

Lincoln, Abraham

Abraham Lincoln (February 12, 1809 – April 15, 1865) was the Sixteenth President of the United States, serving from March 4, 1861 until his assassination. As an outspoken opponent of the expansion of slavery in the United States, Lincoln won the Republican Party nomination in 1860 and was elected president later that year. During his term, he helped preserve the United States by leading the defeat of the secessionist Confederate States of America in the American Civil War. He introduced measures that resulted in the abolition of slavery, issuing his Emancipation Proclamation in 1863 and promoting the passage of the Thirteenth Amendment to the Constitution in 1865.

Locke, John

John Locke (August 29, 1632 – October 28, 1704) was an English philosopher. Locke is considered the first of the British Empiricists, but is equally important to social contract theory. His ideas had enormous influence on the development of epistemology and political philosophy, and he is widely regarded as one of the most influential Enlightenment thinkers and contributors to liberal theory. His writings influenced Voltaire and Rousseau, many Scottish Enlightenment thinkers, as well as the American revolutionaries. This influence is reflected in the American Declaration of Independence.

Locke's theory of mind is often cited as the origin for modern conceptions of identity and "the self", figuring prominently in the later works of philosophers such as David Hume, Jean-Jacques Rousseau and Immanuel Kant. Locke was the first philosopher to define the self through a continuity of "consciousness". He also postulated that the mind was a "blank slate" or "tabula rasa"; that is, contrary to Cartesian or Christian philosophy, Locke maintained that people are born without innate ideas.

Long, Huey

Huey Pierce Long, Jr. (August 30, 1893 – September 10, 1935) nicknamed **The Kingfish**, was an American politician from the U.S. state of Louisiana. A Democrat, he was noted for his radical populist policies. He served as Governor of Louisiana from 1928 to 1932 and as a U.S. senator from 1932 to 1935. Though a backer of Franklin D. Roosevelt in the 1932 presidential election, Long split with Roosevelt in June 1933 and allegedly planned to mount his own presidential bid.

Long created the Share Our Wealth program in 1934, with the motto "Every Man a King", proposing new wealth redistribution measures and the form of a net asset tax on large corporations and individuals of great wealth to curb poverty and crime resulting from the Great Depression. He was an ardent critic of the Federal Reserve System.

Charismatic and immensely popular for his social reform programs and willingness to take forceful action, Long was accused by his opponents of dictatorial tendencies for his near-total control of the state government. At the height of his popularity, the colorful and flamboyant Long was shot on September 8, 1935, at the Louisiana State Capitol in Baton Rouge; he died two days later at the age of 42. His last words were reportedly, "God, don't let me die. I have so much left to do."

Longfellow, Henry Wadsworth

Henry Wadsworth Longfellow (February 27, 1807 – March 24, 1882) was an American poet whose works include "Paul Revere's Ride", "A Psalm of Life", "The Song of Hiawatha", "Evangeline", and "Christmas Bells". He also wrote the first American translation of Dante Alighieri's "Divine Comedy" and was one of the five members of the group known as the Fireside Poets. Longfellow was born and raised in the region of Portland, Maine. He attended university at an early age at Bowdoin College in Brunswick, Maine. After several journeys overseas, Longfellow settled for the last forty-five years of his life in Cambridge, Massachusetts.

Loren, Sophia

Sophia Loren (born September 20, 1934) is a motion picture and stage, Academy Award-winning actress and sex symbol. She is widely considered to be the most popular Italian actress of her time

Louis, Joe

Joseph Louis Barrow (May 13, 1914 – April 12, 1981), best known as **Joe Louis** and nicknamed **The Brown Bomber**, a native of Detroit, Michigan, is considered to be one of the greatest heavyweight boxing champions that ever lived. He held the title for over 11 years, recording 25 successful defenses of the title. In 2003, *Ring Magazine* rated Joe Louis No. 1 on the list of 100 greatest punchers of all time. In 2005, Louis was named the greatest heavyweight of all time by the International Boxing Research Organization., He participated in 27 heavyweight championship fights, a record which still stands.

Lowell, James Russell

James Russell Lowell (b. 22 February 1819, Cambridge, Massachusetts – d. 12 August 1891, Cambridge, Massachusetts) was an American Romantic poet, critic, satirist, diplomat, and abolitionist.

Luther, Martin

Martin Luther (November 10, 1483 – February 18, 1546) was a German monk, theologian, and Protestant Reformer. He is often considered the founder of Protestantism.

Luther's theology challenged the authority of the papacy by holding that the Bible is the sole source of religious authority and that all baptized Christians are a general priesthood. According to Luther, salvation was attainable only by faith in Jesus as the Messiah, a faith unmediated by the church. These ideas helped to inspire the Protestant Reformation and changed the course of Western civilization.

Luther's translation of the Bible into the German vernacular, making it more accessible to ordinary people, had a tremendous impact on the church and on German culture. The translation also furthered the development of a standard version of the German language, added several principles to the art of translation, and influenced the translation of the English King James Bible. His hymns inspired the development of congregational singing within Christianity. His marriage to Katharina von Bora set a model for the practice of clerical marriage within Protestantism.

Macaulay, Thomas Babington

Thomas Babington Macaulay, 1st Baron Macaulay, PC (25 October 1800 – 28 December 1859) was a nineteenth-century English poet, historian and Whig politician and Member of Parliament for Edinburgh. He wrote extensively as an essayist and reviewer, and on British history.

The son of Zachary Macaulay, a Scottish Highlander who became a colonial governor and abolitionist, Thomas was born in Leicestershire, England, and educated at Trinity College, Cambridge. Macaulay was noted as a child prodigy. As a toddler, gazing out the window from his cot at the chimneys of a local factory, he is reputed to have put the question to his mother: "Does the smoke from those chimneys come from the fires of hell?" Whilst at Cambridge he wrote much poetry and won several prizes. In 1825 he published a prominent essay on Milton in the Edinburgh Review. In 1826 he was called to the bar but showed more interest in a political than a legal career.

Macauley, Ed

Charles Edward "Ed" Macauley (born March 22, 1928 in St. Louis, Missouri) is a former professional basketball player.

Macauley spent his prep school days at St. Louis University High School, then went on to Saint Louis University, where his team won the NIT championship in 1948. He was named the AP Player of the Year in 1949.

Macauley played in the NBA with the St. Louis Bombers, Boston Celtics, and St. Louis Hawks. Macauley was named MVP of the first NBA All-Star Game (he played in the first seven), and was named to the NBA's All-NBA First Team three consecutive seasons. He was named to the All-NBA second team once, in 1953 – 54 – the same season he led the league in field goal percentage. Macauley's trade (with Cliff Hagan) to St. Louis brought Bill Russell to the Celtics. Macauley scored 11,234 points in ten NBA seasons and was inducted into the Basketball Hall of Fame in 1960. He also has a star on the St. Louis Walk of Fame.

Machiavelli, Niccolò

Niccolò di Bernardo dei Machiavelli (May 3, 1469 – June 21, 1527) was an Italian diplomat, political philosopher, musician, poet, and playwright. He is a figure of the Italian Renaissance and a central figure of its political component, most widely known for his treatises on realist political theory (*The Prince*) on the one hand and republicanism (*Discourses on Livy*) on the other. These two written works – plus his *History of Florence* commissioned by the Medici family – were published posthumously in 1531. After the ousting and execution of Savonarola, the Great Council elected Machiavelli as the second chancellor of the Republic of Florence in June of 1498.

MacIver, Robert Morrison

Robert Morrison MacIver (April 17, 1882 – June 15, 1970) was a U.S. (Scottish-born) sociologist. Born in North Beach Street, Stornoway, Isle of Lewis, he graduated from the Universities of Edinburgh and Oxford. MacIver was a University Lecturer at the

University of Aberdeen. He left Aberdeen for a post in Toronto in 1915, and remained there – doing wartime administrative work as well as teaching political philosophy, until moving to Barnard College of the University of Columbia in 1927. He was Lieber Professor there, 1929 – 1950. In his – rather long – period of formal education he had never made any formal, academically supervised study of sociology, yet his distinguished work in sociology and in critical discussion of crucial issues of the interpretation of research data, and issues of the state, society and community, were distinguished on his acumen, his philosophical understanding, and extensive study of the major pioneering works of Durkheim, Toennies, Max and Alfred Weber, George Simmel et al., in the British Museum Library, London, while resident as a student in Oxford.

Magrane, Joe

Joseph David Magrane (born July 2, 1964 in Des Moines, Iowa) was a Major League Baseball pitcher and is currently color commentary broadcaster for the the MLB Network. He was previously color commentator for the Tampa Bay Devil Rays, teamed with play-by-play announcer Dewayne Staats.

During his rookie season he helped the Cardinals win the 1987 NL Pennant. He also led the National League in Hit Batsmen.

He led the National League in ERA (2.18) in 1988.

He finished 4th in voting for the 1989 NL MVP for having an 18-9 Win-Loss record, 34 Games, 33 Games Started, 9 Complete Games, 3 Shutouts, 1 Game Finished, 234, 2/3 Innings, 219 Hits Allowed, 81 Runs Allowed, 76 Earned Runs Allowed, 5 Home Runs Allowed, 72 Walks, 127 Strikeouts, 14 Wild Pitches, 971 Batters Faced, 7 Intentional Walks, 5 Balks and a 2.91 ERA.

An injured elbow in 1990 cost him almost all of the next two seasons and most of his effectiveness, and Magrane never really regained his early form. He did win 11 games between the St. Louis and California ball clubs in 1993, but could not muster more than 2 wins or 74 innings pitched in any other season until his retirement in 1996 at the relatively early age of 32.

Mailer, Norman

Norman Kingsley Mailer (January 31, 1923 – November 10, 2007) was an American novelist, journalist, playwright, screenwriter, and film director.

Along with Truman Capote, Joan Didion, and Tom Wolfe, Mailer is considered an innovator of creative nonfiction, a genre sometimes called New Journalism, but which covers the essay to the nonfiction novel. He was awarded the Pulitzer Prize twice and the National Book Award once. In 1955, Mailer, together with Ed Fancher and Dan Wolf, first published *The Village Voice*, which began as an arts-and politics-oriented weekly newspaper initially distributed in Greenwich Village. In 2005, he won the Medal for Distinguished Contribution to American Letters from The National Book Foundation.

Mantle, Mickey

Mickey Charles Mantle (October 20, 1931 – August 13, 1995) was an American baseball player who was inducted into the National Baseball Hall of Fame in 1974.

He played his entire 18-year major-league professional career for the New York Yankees, winning 3 American League MVP titles and playing for 16 All-Star teams. Mantle played on 12 pennant winners and 7 World Championship clubs. He still holds the records for most World Series home runs (18), RBIs (40), runs (42), walks (43), extra-base hits (26), and total bases (123).

Marquis, Don

Don Marquis (July 29, 1878 Walnut, Illinois – December 29, 1937 New York City) was an American humorist, journalist, and author. He was variously a novelist, poet, cartoonist, newspaper columnist, and playwright. He is best remembered for creating the characters "Archy" and "Mehitabel", supposed authors of humorous verse.

On August 23, 1943, the United States Navy christened a Liberty ship, the USS Don Marquis (IX-215), in his memory.

Martial

Marcus Valerius Martialis, (40 – 104) known in English as **Martial**, was a Latin poet from Hispania (the Iberian Peninsula) best known for his twelve books of Epigrams, published in Rome between AD 86 and 103, during the reigns of the emperors Domitian, Nerva and Trajan. In these short, witty poems he cheerfully satirises city life and the scandalous activities of his acquaintances, and romanticizes his provincial upbringing. He wrote a total of 1,561 – 1,235 of which are in elegiac couplets. He is considered the creator of the modern epigram.

Martin, Dean

Dean Martin (born **Dino Paul Crocetti**, June 7, 1917 – December 25, 1995) was an American singer, film actor, and comedian. He was one of the most famous music artists in the 1950s and 1960s. His hit singles included the songs "Memories Are Made Of This", "That's Amore", "Everybody Loves Somebody", "Mambo Italiano", "Sway", "Volare" and "Ain't That a Kick in the Head". He was a major star in all four areas of show business: concert stage, recordings, motion pictures, and television.

Marx, Groucho

Julius Henry "Groucho" Marx (October 2, 1890 – August 19, 1977) was an American comedian and film star. He is famed as a master of wit. He made 15 feature films with his siblings, the Marx Brothers, and also had a successful solo career, most notably as the host of the radio and television game show, *You Bet Your Life*. He had a distinctive image, which included a heavy greasepaint moustache and eyebrows and glasses.

Maugham, W. Somerset

William Somerset Maugham, CH (January 25, 1874 – December 16, 1965) was an English playwright, novelist, and short story writer. He was one of the most popular authors of his era, and reputedly the highest paid of his profession during the 1930s.

Meir, Golda

Golda Meir (born **Goldie Mabovitch**, May 3, 1898 – December 8, 1978, known as **Golda Myerson** from 1917 – 1956) was the fourth prime minister of the State of Israel. After serving as the Minister of Labour and Foreign Minister, Golda Meir became Prime Minister of Israel on March 17, 1969. She was described as the "Iron Lady" of Israeli politics years before the epithet became associated with British prime minister, Margaret Thatcher. David Ben-Gurion used to call her "the only man in the Cabinet". Meir was Israel's first woman prime minister and the third woman in the world to hold this office.

Menander

Menander (ca. 342 – 291 BC), Greek dramatist, the chief representative of the New Comedy, was born in Athens. He was the son of well-to-do parents; his father Diopeithes is identified by some with the Athenian general and governor of the Thracian Chersonese known from the speech of Demosthenes *De Chersoneso*. He presumably derived his taste for the comic drama from his uncle Alexis.

He was the friend, associate, and perhaps pupil of Theophrastus, and was on intimate terms with Demetrius of Phalerum. He also enjoyed the patronage of Ptolemy Soter, the son of Lagus, who invited him to his court.

Menander was the author of more than a hundred comedies, but only won the prize at Lenaia eight times. His rival in dramatic art (and in the affections of Glycera) was Philemon, who appears to have been more popular. Menander, however, believed himself to be the better dramatist, and, according to Aulus Gellius, used to ask Philemon: "Don't you feel ashamed whenever you gain a victory over me?"

Mencken, H. L.

Henry Louis (H. L.) Mencken (September 12, 1880, Baltimore – January 29, 1956, Baltimore, Maryland), was an American journalist, essayist, magazine editor, satirist, acerbic critic of

American life and culture, and a student of American English. Known as the "Sage of Baltimore", he is regarded as one of the most influential American writers and prose stylists of the first half of the 20th century.

Mencken is perhaps best remembered today for *The American Language*, a multi-volume study of how the English language is spoken in the United States and his satirical reporting on the Scopes trial, which is credited for naming the "Monkey" trial.

Montesquieu, Charles de Secondat, baron de

Charles-Louis de Secondat, baron de La Brède et de Montesquieu (January 18, 1689 in Bordeaux – February 10, 1755), was a French social commentator and political thinker who lived during the Era of the Enlightenment. He is famous for his articulation of the theory of separation of powers, taken for granted in modern discussions of government and implemented in many constitutions throughout the world. He was largely responsible for the popularization of the terms feudalism and Byzantine Empire.

Moore, Roger

Sir Roger George Moore KBE (born 14 October 1927) is an English actor. He may be best known for portraying two British action heroes, Simon Templar in the television series *The Saint* from 1962 to 1969, and James Bond in seven films from 1973 to 1985. He has been a UNICEF ambassador since 1991.

Mull, Martin

Martin Mull (born August 18, 1943) is an American actor who has starred in his own TV sitcom and acted in prominent films. He is also a comedian, painter and recording artist.

Munro, Hector Hugh

Hector Hugh Munro (December 18, 1870 – November 14, 1916) better known by the pen name **Saki**, was a British writer, whose witty and sometimes macabre stories satirized Edwardian society and culture. He is considered a master of the short story and is often compared to O. Henry and Dorothy Parker. His tales feature delicately drawn characters and finely judged narratives. "The Open Window" may be his most famous, with a closing line ("Romance at short notice was her speciality") that has entered the lexicon.

In addition to his short stories (which were first published in newspapers, as was the custom of the time, and then collected into several volumes) he also wrote a full-length play, *The Watched Pot*, in collaboration with Charles Maude; two one-act plays: a historical study, *The Rise of the Russian Empire*, the only book published under his own name; a short novel, *The Unbearable Bassington*; the episodic *The Westminster Alice* (a Parliamentary parody of *Alice in Wonderland*), and *When William Came*, subtitled *A Story of London Under the Hohenzollerns*, an early alternative history. He was influenced by Oscar Wilde, Lewis Carrroll, and Kipling, and himself influenced A. A. Milne, Noel Coward, and P. G. Wodehouse.

Namath, Joe

Joseph William Namath (born May 31, 1943, Beaver Falls, Pennsylvania), also known as **Broadway Joe**, was an American football quarterback for the University of Alabama under legendary coach Paul "Bear" Bryant from 1962 – 64, and in the American Football League and National Football League during the 1960s and '70s. Namath played for the New York Jets for most of his professional career, finishing his career with the Los Angeles Rams. He was later elected to the Hall of Fame.

Nash, Ogden

Frederic Ogden Nash (August 19, 1902 – May 19, 1971) was an American poet best known for writing pithy and funny light verse.

Nathan, George Jean

George Jean Nathan (February 14, 1882 – April 8, 1958) was an American drama critic and editor. Nathan was born in Fort Wayne, Indiana. He graduated from Cornell University in 1904, where he was a member of the Quill and Dagger society.

Noted for the erudition and cynicism of his reviews, Nathan was an early champion of Eugene O'Neill. Together with H.L. Mencken, he co-edited the magazine *The Smart Set* from 1914 and co-founded The *American Mercury* in 1924. He was also a founder and an editor (1932 – 35) of the *American Spectator*, and after 1943 he wrote a syndicated column for the *New York Journal-American*.

Over the years, Nathan's criticisms were published in *Mr. George Jean Nathan Presents* (1917), *The Critic and the Drama* (1922), *The Testament of a Critic* (1931), *Since Ibsen* (1933), *Passing Judgments* (1935), *The World of George Jean Nathan* (1952), and *The Magic Mirror* (1960). Nathan's philosophy of criticism is laid out in *Autobiography of an Attitude* (1925).

Nepos, Cornelius

Cornelius Nepos (c. 100 – 24 BC) was a Roman biographer. Supposedly he was born at Hostilia, a village in Cisalpine Gaul not far from Verona. His Gallic origin is attested by Ausonius, and Pliny the Elder calls him *Padi accola* (a dweller on the River Po, *Natural History* III.22). He was a friend of Catullus, who dedicates his poems to him, Cicero and Titus Pomponius Atticus. Eusebius places him in the fourth year of the reign of Augustus, which is supposed to be when he began to attract critical acclaim by his writing. Pliny the Elder notes he died in the reign of Augustus (*Natural History* IX.39, X.23).

Nettles, Graig

Graig Nettles (born August 20, 1944, in San Diego, California) is a former Major League Baseball third baseman and left-handed batter who played for the Minnesota Twins (1967 – 69), Cleveland Indians (1970 – 72), New York Yankees (1973 – 83), San Diego Padres (1984 – 86), Atlanta Braves (1987) and Montreal Expos (1988). He played collegiate baseball with the Aztecs of San Diego State University.

Nettles, known as Puff to fans and teammates, was one of the best defensive third basemen of all time, and despite his relatively low career batting average, he was an excellent offensive contributor, setting an American League record for career home runs by a third baseman.

Niebuhr, Reinhold

Karl Paul Reinhold Niebuhr (June 21, 1892 – June 1, 1971) was a Protestant theologian best know for his study of the task of relating the Christian faith to the reality of modern politics and diplomacy. He is a crucial contributor to modern just war thinking.

Nietzsche, Friedrich

Friedrich Wilhelm Nietzsche (October 15, 1844 – August 25, 1900) was a German philosopher. He wrote critiques of religion, morality, contemporary culture, philosophy, and science, using a distinctive style and displaying a fondness for aphorism. Nietzsche's influence remains substantial within and beyond philosophy, notably in existentialism and postmodernism. His style, and radical questioning of the value and objectivity of truth, raise considerable problems of interpretation, generating an extensive secondary literature in both continental and analytic philosophy. Nonetheless, his key ideas include interpreting tragedy as an affirmation of life, an eternal recurrence that has fallen into numerous interpretations, a reversal of Platonism, and a repudiation of Christianity as it was in the 19th century.

Nixon, Richard

Richard Milhous Nixon (January 9, 1913 – April 22, 1994) was the thirty-seventh President of the United States serving from 1969 until his resignation in 1974. Prior to being elected President, Nixon served as the thirty-sixth Vice President of the United States in the administration of Dwight D. Eisenhower from 1953 to 1961. Nixon is the only person to be elected twice to the offices of the presidency and the vice presidency, and is the only president to have resigned the office. During the Second World War, he served as a Navy lieutenant commander in the Pacific, before being elected to the Congress, and later serving as Vice President. After an unsuccessful presidential run in 1960, Nixon was elected in 1968.

Under President Nixon, the United States followed a foreign policy marked by détente with the Soviet Union and by the opening of diplomatic relations with the People's Republic of

China. Domestically, his administration faced resistance to the Vietnam War. As a result of the Watergate scandal, Nixon resigned the presidency in the face of likely impeachment by the United States House of Representatives and conviction by the Senate. His successor, Gerald Ford, issued a controversial pardon for any federal crimes Nixon may have committed.

Nixon suffered a stroke on April 18, 1994 and died four days later at the age of 81.

Onassis, Aristotle

Aristotelis Sokratis (also **Ari**) **Onassis** (January 15, 1906 – March 15, 1975) was the most famous shipping magnate of the 20th century.

Onassis was born in Smyrna, Ottoman Empire (now Izmir, Turkey) to a middle-class Greek family. At the time of his birth, Smyrna had a very significant and prosperous Greek population. After being briefly occupied by Greece (1919 – 1922) in the aftermath of the allied victory in World War I, the city was re-captured by Turkey; the Onassis family holdings were lost, causing them to move to Greece as refugees. In 1923, Aristotle Onassis left his country to go to Argentina with allegedly only $63. After difficult beginnings, he revived the family's tobacco business. In 1925, he received Argentinian and Greek citizenships. After engaging in many different entrepreneurial activities with determination and passion for success, he finally managed to become a world-class businessman making his first million by the age of 25, owning commercial ships, tankers and whalers. In 1954, the FBI investigated Onassis for fraud against the U.S. government. He was charged with violating the citizenship provision of the shipping laws which require that all ships displaying the U.S. flag be owned by U.S. citizens. Onassis entered a guilty plea and paid $7 million. He founded Olympic Airways (today Olympic Airlines), the Greek national carrier, in 1957.

Orben, Robert

Robert Orben (born March 4, 1927) is an American magician and professional comedy writer. He is also an author of books for magicians. He wrote a book called *Speaker's Handbook of Humor*.

Robert Orben published his first gag book at the age of 18 in 1946, when he was working in Stuart Robson Jr.'s (stage manager for Florenz Ziegfeld) conjuror's shop in New York. Professional magicians would use his gags to add humor to their acts; comedians also came into magic stores, for props and books, as there were no comedy stores or resources as such at that time.

When Robert Orben wrote his first gag book, *Encyclopedia of Patter*, it proved very popular, and he started publishing more books of gags, complete with sketches, ad libs, bits of business and routines. Titles included *Patter Parade*, *Laugh Package*, *Sight Bits*, and *Screamline Comedy*.

O'Rourke, P. J.

Patrick Jake O'Rourke (born November 14, 1947 in Toledo, Ohio) is an American political satirist, journalist, and writer. O'Rourke is the H. L. Mencken Research Fellow at the Cato Institute and is a regular correspondent for *The Atlantic Monthly*, *The American Spectator*, and *The Weekly Standard*, and frequent panelist on National Public Radio's game show *Wait Wait...Don't Tell Me!* He is perhaps best known in the United Kingdom as the face of a long-running series of television advertisements for British Airways in the 1990s.

He is the author of 13 books, most recently *On The Wealth of Nations*, a commentary on Adam Smith's *An Inquiry into the Nature and Causes of the Wealth of Nations* (and the first in *The Atlantic Monthly's* "Books That Changed The World" series). According to a *60 Minutes* profile, he is also the most quoted living man in the *The Penguin Dictionary of Modern Humorous Quotations*.

Orwell, George

Eric Arthur Blair (25 June 1903 – 21 January 1950), known by the pen name **George Orwell**, was an English author and journalist. Noted as a novelist and critic as well as a political and cultural commentator, Orwell is among the most widely admired English-language essayists of the 20th century. He is best known for two novels critical of totalitarianism in general, and Stalinism in particular: *Animal Farm* and *Nineteen Eighty-Four*. Both were written and published towards the end of his life.

Ovid

Publius Ovidius Naso (March 20, 43 BC – 17 AD) was a Roman poet known to the English-speaking world as **Ovid** who wrote on many topics, including love, abandoned women and mythological transformations. Ranked alongside Virgil and Horace as one of the three canonical poets of Latin literature, Ovid was generally considered a great master of the elegiac couplet. His poetry, much imitated during Late Antiquity and the Middle Ages, had a decisive influence on European art and literature for centuries.

Paine, Thomas

Thomas Paine (Thetford, England, 29 January 1737 – June 1809, New York City, U.S.) was an English pamphleteer, revolutionary, radical, classical liberal and intellectual. Born in Great Britain, he lived and worked there until his late thirties, when he migrated to the American colonies just in time to take part in the American Revolution. His main contribution was as the author of the powerful, widely read pamphlet, *Common Sense* (1776), advocating independence for the American Colonies from the Kingdom of Great Britain, and of *The American Crisis*, supporting the Revolution.

Later, Paine was a great influence on the French Revolution. He wrote the *Rights of Man* (1791) as a guide to the ideas of the Enlightenment. Despite an inability to speak French, he was elected to the French National Assembly in 1792. Regarded as an ally of the Girondists, he was seen with increasing disfavour by the Montagnards and in particular by Robespierre.

Paine was arrested in Paris and imprisoned in December 1793; he was released in 1794. He became notorious with his book, *The Age of Reason* (1793 – 94), which advocated deism and took issue with Christian doctrines. While in France, he also wrote a pamphlet titled *Agrarian Justice* (1795), which discussed the origins of property and introduced a concept that is similar to a guaranteed minimum income.

Paine remained in France during the early Napoleonic era, but condemned Napoleon's moves towards dictatorship, calling him "the completest charlatan that ever existed". Paine remained in France until 1802, when he returned to America on an invitation from Thomas Jefferson, who had been elected president.

Paine died at 59 Grove Street in Greenwich Village, New York City, on the morning of June 8, 1809. He was 72.

Park, Brad

Douglas Bradford (Brad) Park (born July 6, 1948 in Toronto, Ontario) was an NHL ice hockey player in the National Hockey League (NHL) and is a member of the Hockey Hall of Fame. He played for the New York Rangers, Boston Bruins and Detroit Red Wings.

Park was drafted by the New York Rangers in the first round (2nd overall) in the 1966 NHL Amateur Draft and, after a brief stint with the minor-league Buffalo Bisons of the AHL, began playing for the Rangers in 1968. He quickly became the Rangers' best defenceman and drew comparisons with the great Bobby Orr. His offensive skill, stickhandling and pugnacity attracted much attention from fans.

Park was made the assistant captain of the Rangers and briefly served as their captain. In 1972 Park led his team to the Stanley Cup finals but lost to Orr and the Boston Bruins. That same year he was the runner-up for the Norris Trophy and was named MVP in the 1972 Summit Series.

Parker, Dorothy

Dorothy Parker (August 22, 1893 – June 7, 1967) was an American writer and poet, best known for her caustic wit, wisecracks, and sharp eye for 20th century urban foibles.

From a conflicted and unhappy childhood, Parker rose to acclaim, both for her literary output in such venues as *The New Yorker* and as a founding member of the Algonquin Round Table, a group she would later disdain. Following the breakup of that circle, Parker traveled to Hollywood to pursue screenwriting. Her successes there, including two Academy Award nominations, would eventually be curtailed, as her involvement in left-wing politics would lead to a place on the infamous Hollywood blacklist.

Parker survived three marriages (two to the same man) and several suicide attempts, but grew increasingly dependent on alcohol. Although she would come to dismiss her own talents and deplore her reputation as a "wisecracker", her literary output and her sparkling wit have endured long past her death.

Parton, Dolly

Dolly Rebecca Parton (born January 19, 1946) is a Grammy Award-winning country music singer/songwriter, composer, author, actress and philanthropist. She remains one of the most successful female country artists in history, with 25 number-one singles (a record for a female country artist) and 41 top-10 country albums (a record for any country artist).

Peale, Norman Vincent

Dr. Norman Vincent Peale (May 31, 1898 – December 24, 1993) was a Protestant preacher and author (most notably of *The Power of Positive Thinking*) and a progenitor of the theory of "positive thinking".

Peter, Laurence J.

Dr. Laurence J. Peter (September 16, 1919 – January 12, 1990) was an educator and "hierarchiologist", best known to the general public for the formulation of the Peter Principle.

He was born in Vancouver, British Columbia, and began his career as a teacher in 1941. He received the degree of Doctor of Education from Washington State University in 1963.

He became widely famous in 1968, on the publication of *The Peter Principle*, in which he states: "In a hierarchy every employee tends to rise to his level of incompetence."

Phaedrus

Phaedrus (c. 15 BC – c. AD 50), Roman fabulist, was probably a Thracian slave, born in Pydna of Macedonia (Roman province) and lived in the reigns of Augustus, Tiberius, Gaius and Claudius. He is recognized as the first writer to latinize entire books of fables, using the iambic metre Greek prose of the Aesop tales.

Picasso, Pablo

Pablo Ruiz Picasso (October 25, 1881 – April 8, 1973), often referred to simply as **Picassso**, was a Spanish painter and sculptor. His full name is **Pablo Diego José Francisco de Paula Juan Nepomuceno María de los Remedios Cipriano de la Santísima Trinidad Clito Ruiz y Picasso**. One of the most recognized figures in 20th century art, he is best known as the co-founder, along with Georges Braque, of cubism.

Plato

Plato (Greek: *plátōn,* "wide, broad-browed")(424/423 BC – 348/347 BC), was a Classical Greek philosopher. Together with his teacher, Socrates, and his student, Aristotle, Plato helped to lay the philosophical foundations of Western culture. Plato was also a mathematician, writer of philosophical dialogues, and founder of the academy in Athens, the first institution of higher learning in the western world. Plato was originally a student of Socrates, and was as much influenced by his thinking as by what he saw as his teacher's unjust death.

Plato's brilliance as a writer and thinker can be witnessed by reading his Socratic dialogues. Some of the dialogues, letters, and other works that are ascribed to him are considered spurious. Interestingly, although there is little question that Plato lectured at the Academy that he founded, the pedagogical function of his dialogues, if any, is not known with certainty. The dialogues have since Plato's time been used to teach a range of subjects, mostly including philosophy, logic, rhetoric, mathematics, and other subjects about which he wrote.

Plautus, Titus Maccius

Titus Maccius Plautus (c. 254 – 184 BCE), commonly know as **Plautus**, was a Roman playwright. His comedies are among the earliest surviving intact works in Latin literature. He is also one of the earliest pioneers of musical theater. The word **Plautine** is used to refer to Plautus's works or works similar to or influenced by his.

Pliny the Younger

Gaius or **Caius Plinius Caecilius Decundus**, born Gaius or Caius Plinius Caecilius (62 – ca. 113), better know as **Pliny the Younger**, was a lawyer, a remarkable writer, an author and a natural philosopher of Ancient Rome.

Poe, Edgar Allan

Edgar Allan Poe (January 19, 1809 – October 7, 1849) was an American poet, short-story writer, editor, and literary critic, and is considered part of the American Romantic Movement. Best known for his tales of mystery and the macabre, Poe was one of the earliest American practitioners of the short story and invented the detective-fiction genre. He is credited with contributing to the emerging genre of science fiction. He was the first well-known American writer to try to earn a living through writing alone, resulting in a financially difficult life and career.

Pope, Alexander

Alexander Pope (21 May 1688 – 30 May 1744) is generally regarded as the greatest English poet of the early eighteenth century, best known for his satirical verse and for his translation of Homer. He is the third most frequently quoted writer in the English language, after Shakespeare and Tennyson. Pope was a master of the heroic couplet.

Pope Saint John XXIII

Pope Saint John XXIII (Latin: *Ioannes PP.XXIII*; Italian: *Giovanni XXIII*), born **Angelo Giuseppe Roncalli** (November 25, 1881 June 3, 1963), was elected as the 261st Pope of the Roman Catholic Church and sovereign of Vatican City on October 28, 1958. He called the Second Vatican Council (1962 – 1965) but did not live to see it to completion, dying on June 3, 1963, two months after the completion of his final encyclical, *Pacem in Terris*. He was beatified on September 3, 2000, along with Pope Pius IX, the first popes since Pope St. Pius X to receive this honor. His feast day is October 11 in the Catholic Church, the day that Vatican II's first session opened. He is also commemorated on June 3 by the Evangelical Lutheran Church in America and on June 4 by the Anglican Church of Canada. He was canonised alongside John Paul II on 27 April 2014.

In Italy he is remembered with the affectionate appellative of "Il Papa Buono" ("The Good Pope").

Presley, Elvis

Elvis Aaron Presley (January 8, 1935 – August 16, 1977) was an American singer, musician and actor. He is a cultural icon, often known as **"The King of Rock 'n' Roll"**, or simply **"The King"**.

Presley began his career as one of the first performers of rockabilly, an uptempo fusion of country and rhythm and blues with a strong back beat. His novel versions of existing songs, mixing "black" and "white" sounds, made him popular – and controversial – as did his uninhibited stage and television performances. He recorded songs in the rock and roll genre, with tracks like "Hound Dog" and "Jailhouse Rock" later embodying the style. Presley had a versatile voice and had unusually wide success encompassing other genres, including gospel, blues, ballads and pop. To date, he is the only performer to have been inducted into four music halls of fame.

In the 1960s, Presley made the majority of his thirty-three movies – mainly poorly reviewed musicals. In 1968, he returned to live music in a television special and thereafter performed across the U.S., notably in Las Vegas. Throughout his career, he set records for concert attendance, television ratings and recordings sales. He is one of the best-selling and most influential artists in the history of popular music. Health problems plagued Presley in later life which, coupled with a punishing tour schedule and addiction to prescription medication, led to his premature death at age 42.

Priestley, J. B.

John Boynton Priestley, OM (born 13 September 1894, Bradford, West Riding of Yorkshire, died 14 August 1984, Warwickshire) was an English writer and broadcaster.

By the age of 30 he had established a reputation as a humorous writer and critic. His 1927 novel *Benighted* was adapted into the James Whale film *The Old Dark House* in 1932. His first major success came with a novel, *The Good Companions* (1929) which earned him the James Tait Black Memorial Prize for fiction and made him a national figure. His next novel *Angel Pavement* (1930) further established him as a successful novelist.

Pryor, Richard

Richard Franklin Lennox Thomas Pryor III (December 1, 1940 – December 10, 2005) was an American comedian, actor, and writer.

Pryor was a storyteller known for unflinching examinations of racism and customs in modern life, and was well known for his frequent use of colorful language, vulgarities, and racial epithets such as "nigger", "honky", "cracker", and "motherfucker". He reached a broad audience with his trenchant observations, although public opinion of his act was often divided. He is commonly regarded as the most important stand-up comedian of his time: Jerry Seinfeld called Pryor "the Picasso of our profession." Whoopi Goldberg cited him as her biggest influence, stating: "The major influence was Richard – I want to say those things he's saying." Bob Newhart has called Pryor "the seminal comedian of the last 50 years."

His body of work includes such concert movies and recordings as *Richard Pryor: Live and Smokin'* (1971), *That Nigger's Crazy* (1974), *...Is It Something I Said?* (1975), *Bicentennial Nigger* (1976), *Richard Pryor: Live in Concert* (1979), *Richard Pryor: Live on the Sunset Strip* (1982) and *Richard Pryor: Here and Now*. He also starred in numerous films as an actor, usually in comedies such as *Silver Streak*, but occasionally in dramatic roles, such as Paul Schrader's film *Blue Collar* and epic roles like Gus Gorman from *Superman III* (1983). He also collaborated on many projects with actor Gene Wilder. He won an Emmy |Award in 1973, and five Grammy Awards in 1974, 1975, 1976, 1981, and 1982. In 1974, he also won two American Academy of Humor awards and the Writers Guild of America Award. In 2004, Pryor was voted the greatest stand-up act of all time by Comedy Central.

Puzo, Mario

Mario Gianluigi Puzo (October 15, 1920 – July 2, 1999) was an Italian-American author known for his novels about the Mafia, especially *The Godfather* (1969).

Puzo was born into a poor family of Neapolitan immigrants living in the Hell's Kitchen neighborhood of New York City. Many of his books draw heavily on this heritage. After graduating form the City College of New York, he joined the United States Army Air Forces in World War II. Due to poor eyesight, the military did not let him undertake combat duties but made him a public relations officer stationed in Germany. After the war, he wrote his first book, *The Dark Arena*, which came out in 1955.

His most famous work, *The Godfather*, was first published in 1969 after he had heard anecdotes about Mafia organizations during his time in pulp journalism. The book was later developed into a trilogy of films (*The Godfather*, *The Godfather Part II* and *The Godfather Part III*) directed by Francis Ford Coppola.

Puzo wrote the first draft of the script for the 1974 disaster film *Earthquake*, which he was unable to continue working on due to his commitment to *The Godfather: Part II*. Puzo also co-wrote Richard Donner's *Superman: The Movie* and the original draft for *Superman II*.

Quintilian, Marcus Fabius

Marcus Fabius Quintilianus (ca. 35 – ca. 100) was a Roman rhetorician from Hispania, widely referred to in medieval schools of rhetoric and in Renaissance writing. In English translation, he is usually referred to as **Quintilian**, although the alternate spellings of **Quintillian** and **Quinctilian** are occasionally seen, the latter in older texts.

Quintilian was born ca. 35 in Calagurris (now Calahorra, La

Rioja) in Hispania. His father, a well-educated man, sent him to Rome to study rhetoric early in the reign of Nero.

Rawlings, Marjorie Kinnan

Marjorie Kinnan Rawlings (August 8, 1896 – December 14, 1953) was an American author who lived in rural Florida and wrote novels with rural themes and settings. Her best known work, *The Yearling*, about a boy who adopts an orphaned fawn, won a Pulitzer Prize for fiction in 1939 and was later made into a movie, also known as *The Yearling*. The book was written long before the concept of young-adult fiction, but is now commonly included in teen-reading lists.

Renoir, Pierre-Auguste

Pierre-Auguste Renoir (February 25, 1841 – December 3, 1919) was a French artist who was a leading painter in the development of the Impressionist style. As a celebrator of beauty, and especially feminine sensuality, it has been said that "Renoir is the final representative of a tradition which runs directly from Rubens to Watteau".

Repplier, Agnes

Agnes Repplier (April 1, 1855 – November 15, 1950) was an American essayist born in Philadelphia, Pennsylvania. Her essays are esteemed for their scholarship and wit.

Reston, James

James Barrett Reston (November 3, 1909 – December 6, 1995) (nicknamed "**Scotty**") was a prominent American journalist whose career spanned the mid 1930s to the early 1990s. Associated for many years with *The New York Times*, he became perhaps the most powerful, influential, and widely-read journalist of his era.

Robinson, Sugar Ray

Sugar Ray Robinson (born **Walker Smith Jr.**, May 3, 1921 – April 12, 1989) was a professional boxer. Frequently cited as the greatest boxer of all time, Robinson's performances at the welterweight and middleweight divisions prompted sportswriters to create "pound for pound" rankings, where they compared fighters regardless of weight. He was inducted into the International Boxing Hall of Fame in 1990.

Robinson was 85-0 as an amateur with 69 of those victories coming by way of knockout, 40 in the first round. He turned professional in 1940 at the age of 19 and by 1951 had a professional record of 128-1-2 with 84 knockouts. Robinson held the world welterweight title from 1946 to 1951, and won the world middleweight title in the latter year. He retired in 1952, only to come back two and a half years later and regain the middleweight title in 1955. He then became the first boxer in history to win a divisional world championship five times.

Rochefoucauld, François de La

François VI, duc de La Rochefoucauld, le Prince de Marcillac (September 15, 1613 – March 17, 1680), was a noted French author of maxims and memoirs, as well as an example of the accomplished 17th-century nobleman. He was born in Paris in the Rue des Petits Champs, at a time when the royal court oscillated between aiding the nobility and threatening it. Until 1650, he bore the title of Prince de Marcillac.

Rockefeller, John D.

John Davidson Rockefeller, Sr. (July 8, 1839 – May 23, 1937) was an American industrialist and philanthropist. Rockefeller revolutionized the petroleum industry and defined the structure of modern philanthropy. In 1870, Rockefeller founded the Standard Oil Company and ran it until he retired in the late 1890s. He kept his stock and as gasoline grew in importance, his wealth soared and he became the world's richest man and first U.S. dollar billionaire, and is often regarded as the richest person in history. Standard Oil was convicted in Federal Court of monopolistic practices and broken up in 1911. Rockefeller spent the last 40 years of his life in retirement. His fortune was mainly used to create the modern systematic approach of targeted philanthropy with foundations that had a major effect on medicine, education, and scientific research. His foundations pioneered the development of medical research, and were instrumental in the eradication of hookworm and yellow fever. He was a devoted Northern Baptist and supported many church-based institutions throughout his life.

Rockefeller, Nelson

Nelson Aldrich Rockefeller (July 8, 1908 – January 26, 1979) was the forty-first Vice President of the United States, governor of New York, philanthropist, and businessman.

A leader of the liberal wing of the Republican Party, he was Governor of New York from 1959 to 1973, where he launched many construction and modernization projects. A descendant of one of the world's richest and best known families, he failed repeatedly in his attempts to become president, but he was appointed Vice President in 1974. He served from 1974 to 1977, and did not join the 1976 GOP national ticket with President Gerald Ford. He retired from politics when his term as Vice President was over.

Rodríguez, Juan "Chi-Chi"

Juan Antonio "Chi-Chi" Rodríguez (born October 23, 1935) is a Puerto Rican professional golfer. He was the first Puerto Rican to be inducted into the World Golf Hall of Fame.

Rodríguez was born in Rio Piedras, Puerto Rico into a poor family, one of six siblings. His father used to earn only $18 a week as a laborer and cattle handler. When Rodríguez was only seven years old, he would help the family by earning money as a water carrier on a sugar plantation. One day Juan wandered off, as many children his age do, but into a golf course. When he saw that the caddies were earning more money than him, he decided to become a caddy himself.

Rodríguez would take a branch from a guava tree and turn it into a golf club. Using a metal can as a "golf ball", he would practice what he had seen the "real" golfers do, teaching himself how to play golf. By the time he was nine years old, he was proficient at golf and in 1947 at the age of 12, he scored a remarkable 67.

In 1954, when Rodríguez was 19, he joined the Army. During his breaks, he would visit whichever golf course was nearby, where he continued to perfect his game.

Rodríguez turned professional in 1960. In 1963, at 28, Rodríguez won the Denver Open, which he considers as his favorite win. In total he won eight titles on the PGA Tour between 1963 and 1979. He played on the 1973 U.S. Ryder Cup team.

At first, Rodríguez used to put his hat over the hole whenever he made a birdie or eagle. After he heard that other golfers were complaining about his little act, he decided to try something new. Juan developed his signature "toreador dance", where he would make believe that the birdie was a "bull" and that his putter was a "sword" and he would terminate the "bull". Rodríguez represented Puerto Rico on 12 World Cup teams. In 1986, he won the Hispanic Recognition Award. In 1988, he was named Replica's Hispanic Man of the Year.

Rodríguez became eligible to play on the Senior PGA Tour (now known as the Champions Tour) in 1985 and did so for many years with great success, accumulating 22 tournament victories between 1986 and 1993. He was the first player on the Senior PGA Tour to win the same event in three consecutive years. He set a tour record with eight consecutive birdies en route to a win at the 1987 Silver Pages Classic.

In 1989, he was voted the Bob Jones Award, the highest honor given by the United States Golf Association in recognition of distinguished sportsmanship in golf. In 1991, he lost an 18-hole playoff to a legendary Jack Nicklaus in the U.S. Senior Open. In 1992, Juan "Chi-Chi" Rodríguez was inducted into the World Golf Hall of Fame, the first Puerto Rican so honored.

Rogers, Ginger

Ginger Rogers (born **Virginia Katherine McMath**, July 16, 1911 – April 25, 1995) was an Academy Award-winning American film and stage actress and singer. In a film career spanning fifty years she made a total of seventy-three films, and is now principally celebrated for her role as Fred Astaire's romantic interest and dancing partner in a series of ten Hollywood musical films that revolutionized the genre.

Rogers, Will

William Penn Adair "Will" Rogers (November 4, 1879 – August 15, 1935) was a Cherokee-American cowboy, comedian, humorist, social commentator, vaudeville performer and actor.

Known as Oklahoma's favorite son, Rogers was born to a prominent Indian Territory family and learned to ride horses and use a lariat so well that he was listed in the Guinness Book of World Records for throwing three ropes at once – one around the neck of a horse, another around the horse's rider, and a third around all four legs of the horse. He ultimately traveled around the world three times, made movies (50 silent films and 21 "talkies"), wrote more than 4,000 nationally-syndicated newspaper columns, and became a world-famous figure.

By the mid-1930s, Rogers was adored by the American people, and was the top-paid movie star in Hollywood at the time. On an around-the-world trip with aviator Wiley Post, Rogers died when their small airplane crashed near Barrow, Alaska Territory in 1935.

Roosevelt, Franklin D.

Franklin Delano Roosevelt (January 30, 1882 – April 12, 1945), often referred to by his initials **FDR**, was the thirty-second President of the United States. Elected to four terms in office, he served from 1933 to 1945, and is the only U.S. president to have served more than two terms. He was a central figure of the 20th century during a time of worldwide economic crisis and world war.

During the Great Depression of the 1930s, Roosevelt created the New Deal to provide relief for the unemployed, recovery of the economy, and reform of the economic and banking systems. Although recovery of the economy was incomplete until almost 1940, many programs initiated in the Roosevelt administration continue to have instrumental roles in the nation's commerce, such as the FDIC, TVA, and the SEC. One of his most important legacies is the Social Security system.

Roosevelt won four presidential elections in a row, causing a realignment that political scientists call the Fifth Party System.

His aggressive use of an active federal government re-energized the Democratic Party, created a New Deal Coalition which dominated American politics until the late 1960s. He and his wife, Eleanor Roosevelt, remain touchstones for modern American liberalism. Conservatives vehemently fought back, but Roosevelt usually prevailed until he tried to pack the Supreme Court in 1937. Thereafter, the new Conservative coalition successfully ended New Deal expansion; during the war it closed most relief programs like the WPA and Civilian Conservation Corps, arguing that unemployment had disappeared.

After 1938, Roosevelt championed re-armament and led the nation away from isolationism as the world headed into World War II. He provided extensive support to Winston Churchill and the British war effort before the attack on Pearl Harbor pulled the U.S. into the fighting. During the war, Roosevelt, working closely with his aide Harry Hopkins, provided decisive leadership against Nazi Germany and made the United States the principal arms supplier and financier of the Allies who later, alongside the United States, defeated Germany, Italy and Japan. Roosevelt led the United States as it became the Arsenal of Democracy, putting 16 million American men into uniform.

Rostand, Jean

Jean Rostand (October 30, 1894 – September 4, 1977) was a French biologist and philosopher.

Active as an experimental biologist, Rostand became famous for his work as a science writer, as well as a philosopher and an activist. His scientific work covered a variety of biological fields such as amphibian embryology, parthenogenesis and teratogeny, while his literary output extended into popular science, history of science and philosophy.

Rousseau, Jean-Jacques

Jean-Jacques Rousseau, (June 28, 1712 – July 2, 1778) was a philosopher and composer of the Enlightenment whose political philosophy influenced the French Revolution, the development of

both liberal and socialist theory, and the growth of nationalism. With his *Confessions* and other writings, he practically invented modern autobiography and encouraged a new focus on the building of subjectivity that would bear fruit in the work of thinkers as diverse as Hegel and Freud. His novel *Julie, ou la nouvelle Héloïse* was one of the best selling fictional works of the eighteenth century and was important to the development of romanticism. Rousseau also made important contributions to music both as a theorist and a composer.

Runyon, Damon

Damon Runyon (October 4, 1884 – December 10, 1946) was a newspaperman and writer.

He was best known for his short stories celebrating the world of Broadway in New York City that grew out of the Prohibition era. He spun humorous tales of gamblers, hustlers, actors and gangsters; few of whom go by "square" names, preferring instead to be known as "Nathan Detroit", "Big Jule", "Harry the Horse", "Good Time Charley", "Dave the Dude", and so on. These stories were written in a very distinctive vernacular style: a mixture of formal speech and colorful slang, almost always in present tense, and always devoid of contractions.

Russell, Bertrand

Bertrand Arthur William Russell, 3rd Earl Russell, OM, FRS, (18 May 1872 – 2 February 1970), was a Welsh philosopher, historian, logician, mathematician, advocate for social reform, pacifist, and prominent rationalist.

A prolific writer, he was a popularizer of philosophy and a commentator on a large variety of topics. Continuing a family tradition in political affairs, he was a prominent anti-war activist, championing free trade between nations and anti-imperialism. He also co-authored, with Alfred North Whitehead, *Principia Mathematica*, an attempt to ground Mathematics on the laws of Logic. The book has had a considerable influence on Analytic Philosophy.

Safire, William

William L. Safire (December 17, 1929 – September 27, 2009) is an American author, semi-retired columnist, and former journalist and presidential speechwriter.

He is perhaps best known as a long-time syndicated political columnist for *The New York Times* and a regular contributor to "On Language" in the *New York Times Magazine*, a column on popular etymology, new or unusual usages, and other language-related topics.

Saget, Bob

Robert Lane Saget (born May 17, 1956) is an American actor, stand-up comedian, writer, director, producer, and game show host. He is well known for his role as Danny Tanner in the ABC sitcom *Full House* from 1987 to 1995, host of *America's Funniest Home Videos* from 1989 to 1997. Currently he is the host of the NBC game show *1 vs. 100* as well as the narrator of the CBS comedy series *How I Met Your Mother*.

Saget is generally known for his clean-cut, family-friendly television persona from the hit shows *Full House* and *America's Funniest Home Videos*, which have been widely rerun in syndication for over a decade. In contrast, Saget is also known for using edgy humor in his stand-up comedy acts and movies.

Santayana, George

George Santayana (December 16, 1863, Madrid – September 26, 1952, Rome) was a philosopher, essayist, poet, and novelist.

A lifelong Spanish citizen, Santayana was raised and educated in the United States, wrote in English and is generally considered an American man of letters, even though, of his nearly 89 years, he spent only 39 in the U.S. He is perhaps best known as an aphorist, and for the oft-misquoted remark, "Those who cannot remember the past are condemned to repeat it", from *Reason in Common Sense*, the first volume of his *The Life of Reason*.

Sargent, John Singer

John Singer Sargent (January 12, 1856 – April 14, 1925) was the most successful portrait painter of his era, as well as a gifted landscape painter and watercolorist. Sargent was born in Florence, Italy to American parents. He studied in Italy and Germany, and then in Paris under Emile Auguste Carolus-Duran.

Schulz, Charles M.

Charles Monroe Schulz (November 26, 1922 – February 12, 2000) was a 20th-century American cartoonist best known worldwide for his *Peanuts* comic strip.

Scott-Maxwell, Florida

Florida Pier Scott-Maxwell (1883 – 1979) was a writer, playwright, and suffragist who took up a career in analytical psychology in 1933, studying under Carl Jung in both Scotland and England.

(From Penguin group (usa) online.)

Seneca the Elder

Lucius, or **Marcus, Annaeus Seneca**, known as **Seneca the Elder** and **Seneca the Rhetorician** (ca. 54 BC – ca. 39 AD) was a Roman rhetorician and writer, born of a well-to-do equestrian family of Cordoba, Hispania.

His *praenomen* is uncertain, but in any case Marcus is an arbitrary conjecture of Raphael of Volterra. During a lengthy stay on two occasions at Rome, Seneca attended the lectures of famous orators and rhetoricians, to prepare for an official career as an advocate. His ideal orator was Cicero, and Seneca disapproved of the florid tendencies of the oratory of his time.

Shakespeare, William

William Shakespeare (baptized 26 April 1564 – 23 April 1616) was an English poet and playwright, widely regarded as the greatest writer in the English language and the world's pre-eminent dramatist. He is often called England's national poet and the "Bard of Avon" (or simply "The Bard"). His surviving works consist of 38 plays, 154 sonnets, two long narrative poems, and several other poems. His plays have been translated into every major living language and are performed more often than those of any other playwright.

Shakespeare produced most of his known work between 1590 and 1613. His early plays were mainly comedies and histories, genres he raised to the peak of sophistication and artistry by the end of the sixteenth century. Next he wrote mainly tragedies until about 1608, producing plays, such as *Hamlet*, *King Lear*, and *Macbeth*, considered some of the finest in the English language. In his last phase, he wrote tragicomedies and collaborated with other playwrights. Many of his plays were published in editions of varying quality and accuracy during his lifetime, and in 1623, two of his former theatrical colleagues published the First Folio, a collected edition of his dramatic works that included all but two of the plays now recognized as Shakespeare's.

Shaw, George Bernard

George Bernard Shaw (26 July 1856 – 2 November 1950) was a world-famous playwright. Born in Dublin, he moved to London at age twenty and lived in England for the remainder of his life. Shaw's first success was as a music and literary critic, but he was drawn to drama and authored more than sixty plays during his career. Typically his work is leavened by a delightful vein of comedy, but nearly all of it has serious undertones. His plays and prefaces pinpoint institutionalized defects in many aspects of Western culture and suggest reforms. Education, marriage, religion, government, health care, class privilege…All of these were targets, but his prime aim was to free the working class from the abusive exploitation that pervaded the Victorian era. Humor was Shaw's way of making his attacks on the establishment less distressing to his audiences.

Politically an ardent socialist, Shaw wrote many brochures and speeches for the Fabian Society and became an accomplished orator in furtherance of its causes. Those included gaining equal political rights for men and women, alleviating abuses of the working class, rescinding private ownership of productive land, and promoting healthful lifestyles.

Sheridan, Richard Brinsley

Richard Brinsley Sheridan (October 30, 1751 – July 7, 1816) was an Irish playwright and Whig statesman.

Smith, Sydney

Sydney Smith (June 3, 1771, Woodford, Essex, England – February 22, 1845 London), was an English writer and clergyman.

Socrates

Socrates (c. 470 BC – 399 BC), of the deme Alopece of Athens, was a Classical Greek philosopher. He is best known for the creation of Socratic irony and the Socratic Method, or elenchus. Specifically, Socrates is renowned for developing the practice of a philosophical type of pedagogy, in which the teacher asks questions of the student to elicit the best answer, and fundamental insight, on the part of the student.

Socrates is credited with exerting a powerful influence upon the founders of Western philosophy, most particularly Plato and Aristotle, and while Socrates' principal contribution to philosophy is in the field of ethics, he also made important and lasting contributions to the fields of epistemology and logic.

Sowell, Thomas

Thomas Sowell (born June 30, 1930) is an American economist, political writer, and commentator. While often described as a "black conservative", he prefers not to be labeled, and considers himself more libertarian than conservative. He often writes from an economically laissez-faire perspective. He is currently a senior fellow of the Hoover Institution at Stanford University. In 1990, he won the Francis Boyer Award, presented by the American Enterprise Institute. In 2002 he was awarded the National Humanities Medal for prolific scholarship melding history, economics, and political science.

Spinks, Leon

Leon Spinks (born July 11, 1953 in St. Louis, Missouri) is a former boxer. He had an overall record of 26 wins, 17 losses and 3 draws as a professional, with 14 knockout wins. While still an amateur, he also became a member of the United States Marine Corps. Spinks went from being heavyweight champion of the world to being homeless in little more than a decade.

He won the gold medal in the light heavyweight division during the 1976 Summer Olympics in Montreal, alongside brother Michael Spinks, who also won a gold medal in those games. Two years earlier, at the inaugural 1974 World Amateur Boxing Championships in Havana, Cuba, he captured the bronze medal.

Squire, J. C.

Sir John Squire (John Collings Squire) (April 2, 1884 – December 20, 1958) was a British poet, writer, historian, and influential literary editor of the post-World War I period. He also moved in society circles.

Stalin, Joseph

Joseph Vissarionovich Jugashvili (December 18, 1878 – March 5, 1953), better known by his adopted name, **Joseph Stalin** meaning "made of steel", was General Secretary of the Communist Party of the Soviet Union's Central Committee from 1922 until his death in 1953.

During that time, he established the eponymous regime, **Stalinism**. Although Stalin's formal position originally had little significant influence, his office being nominally one of several Central Committee Secretariats, Stalin's increasing control of the Party from 1928 onwards led to his becoming the *de facto* party leader and the dictator of his country, in full control of the Soviet Union and its people. His crash programs of industrialization and collectivization in the 1930s and his campaigns of political repression cost the lives of millions of people. However, it helped industrialize the Soviet union making it a great power by 1931. Only six years later, the Soviet Union had become the second largest industrial nation in the world.

During Stalin's reign, the Soviet Union played a major role in the defeat of Nazi Germany in the Second World War (1939 – 1945) (more commonly known in Russia and post-Soviet republics as the Great Patriotic War). Under Stalin's leadership, the Soviet Union went on to achieve recognition as one of just two superpowers in the post-war era, a status that lasted for nearly four decades after his death.

Stengel, Casey

Charles Dillon "Casey" Stengel (July 30, 1890 – September 29, 1975), nicknamed "The Old Professor", was an American baseball player and manager from the early 1910s into the 1960s. He was born in Kansas City, and was originally nicknamed "Dutch", a common nickname at that time for Americans of German ancestry. After his major league career started, he acquired the nickname "Casey", which originally came from the initials of his hometown ("K. C."), which evolved into "Casey", influenced by the wide popularity of the poem *Casey at the Bat*. In the 1950s, sportswriters dubbed him with yet another nickname, "The Old Professor", for his sharp wit and his ability to talk at length on anything baseball-related.

Stevenson, Adlai

Adlai Ewing Stevenson II (February 5, 1900 – July 14, 1965) was an American politician, noted for his intellectual demeanor and advocacy of liberal causes in the Democratic party. He served one term as governor of Illinois and ran, unsuccessfully, for president against Dwight D. Eisenhower in 1952 and 1956. He served as Ambassador to the United Nations from 1961 to 1965.

Stevenson, Robert Louis

Robert Louis (Balfour) Stevenson (November 13, 1850 – December 3, 1894), was a Scottish novelist, poet, and travel writer, and a leading representative of neo-romanticism in English literature. He was greatly admired by many authors, including Jorge Luis Borges, Ernest Hemingway, Rudyard Kipling and Vladimir Nabokov.

Most modernist writers dismissed him, however, because he was popular and did not write within their narrow definition of literature. It is only recently that critics have begun to look beyond Stevenson's popularity and allow him a place in the Western Canon.

He prepared for a law career but never practiced. He traveled frequently, partly in search of better climates for his weak lungs (possibly due to tuberculosis), which contributed to his death at age 44.

Stewart, James (actor)

James Maitland Stewart (20 May 1908 – 2 July 1997), popularly known as Jimmy Stewart especially in the United States, was an iconic, Academy Award-winning American film and stage actor, best known for his self-effacing screen persona. Over the course of his career, he starred in many films widely considered classics and was nominated for five Oscars, winning one in competition and one life achievement. He also had a noted military career, rising to the rank of Brigadier General in the United States Air Force.

Strachey, Lytton

Giles Lytton Strachey (March 1, 1880 – January 21, 1932) was a British writer and critic. He is best known for establishing a new form of biography in which psychological insight and sympathy are combined with irreverence and wit. His 1921 biography *Queen Victoria* was awarded the James Tait Black Memorial Prize.

Sutton, Don

Donald Howard Sutton (born April 2, 1945) is a former Major League Baseball player and current television sportscaster.

A right-handed pitcher, Sutton played for the Sioux Falls Packers as a minor leaguer, and entered the major league at the age of 21. Don Sutton's major league debut was on April 14, 1966. In the majors, he played 23 years for the Los Angeles Dodgers, Houston Astros, Milwaukee Brewers, Oakland Athletics, and California Angels. He won a total of 324 games, 58 of them shutouts and five of them one-hitters, and he is eighth on baseball's all time strikeout

list with 3,574 K's. He also holds the major league record for number of consecutive losses to one team, having lost 13 straight games to the Chicago Cubs. A 4-time All-Star, Sutton was elected to the Baseball Hall of Fame in 1998.

Swift, Jonathan

Jonathan Swift (November 30, 1667 – October 19, 1745) was an Irish cleric, Dean of St. Patrick's, Dublin, satirist, essayist, political pamphleteer (first for Whigs than for Tories), and poet, famous for works like *Gulliver's Travels*, *A Modest Proposal*, *A Journal to Stella*, *The Drapier's Lettters*, *The Battle of the Books*, and *A Tale of a Tub*. Swift is probably the foremost prose satirist in the English language, and is less well known for his poetry. Swift published all of his works under pseudonyms – such as Lemuel Gulliver, Isaac Bickerstaff, M.B. Drapier – or anonymously. He is also known for being a master of two styles of satire: the Horatian and Juvenalian styles.

Syrus, Publilius

Publilius (less correctly Publius) **Syrus**, (85 – 43 BC), a Latin writer of maxims, flourished in the 1st century BC. He was a native of Syria, and was brought as a slave to Italy, but by his wit and talent he won the favor of his master, who freed and educated him.

His mimes, in which he acted himself, had a great success in the provincial towns of Italy and at the games given by Caesar in 46 BC. Publilius was perhaps even more famous as an improviser, and received from Caesar himself the prize in a contest in which he vanquished all his competitors, including the celebrated Decimus Laberius.

All that remains of his works is a collection of *Sentences* (*Sententiae*), a series of moral maxims in iambic and trochaic verse. This collection must have been made at a very early date, since it was known to Aulus Gellius in the 2nd century AD. Each maxim is comprised of a single verse, and the verses are arranged in alphabetical order according to their initial letters. In the course of time the collection was interpolated with sentences drawn from other writers, especially from apocryphal writings of

Seneca; the number of genuine verses is about 700. They include many pithy sayings, such as the famous *"judex damnatur ubi nocens absolvitur"* ("The judge is condemned when the guilty is acquitted.") adopted as its motto by the *Edinburgh Review*.

Tacitus

Publius (or **Gaius**) **Cornelius Tacitus** (ca. 56 – ca. 117) was a senator and a historian of the Roman Empire. The surviving portions of his two major works – the *Annals* and the *Histories* – examine the reigns of the Roman Emperors Tiberius, Claudius, Nero and those that reigned in the Year of the Four Emperors. These two works span the history of the Roman Empire from the death of Augustus in 14 AD to (presumably) the death of emperor Domitian in 96 AD. There are significant lacunae in the surviving texts.

Talleyrand-Périgord, Charles Maurice de

Charles Maurice de Talleyrand-Périgord, 1ˢᵗ Sovereign Prince de Bénévent (February 2, 1754 – May 17, 1838), *the Prince of Diplomats*, was a French diplomat. He worked successfully from the regime of Louis XVI, through the French Revolution and then under Napoleon I, Louis XVIII and Louis-Philippe. Known since the turn of the 19ᵗʰ century simply by the name **Talleyrand**, he is widely regarded as one of the most versatile and influential diplomats in European history.

Teresa, Mother

Mother Teresa (Albanian: **Agnes Gonxha Bojaxhiu**; August 26, 1910 – September 5, 1997) was a Roman Catholic nun who founded the Missionaries of Charity in Kolkata (Calcutta), India in 1950. For over forty years she ministered to the poor, sick, orphaned, and dying, while guiding the Missionaries of Charity's expansion, first throughout India and then in other countries.

By the 1970s she had become internationally famed as a humanitarian and advocate for the poor and helpless, due in part to a documentary, and book, *Something Beautiful for God* by Malcolm Muggeridge. She won the Nobel Peace Prize in 1979 for her humanitarian work. Mother Teresa's Missionaries of Charity continued to expand, and at the time of her death it was operating 610 missions in 123 countries, including hospices and homes for people with HIV/AIDS, leprosy and tuberculosis, soup kitchens, children's and family counseling programs, orphanages, and schools.

Thomas, Dylan

Dylan Marlais Thomas (27 October 1914 – 9 November 1953) was a Welsh poet. He is regarded by many as one of the 20th century's most influential poets.

In addition to poetry, Thomas also wrote short stories and scripts for film and radio, with the latter frequently performed by Thomas himself. His public readings, particularly in America, won him great acclaim; his booming, at times ostentatious, voice with a subtle Welsh lilt, became almost as famous as his works. His best known works include *Under Milk Wood* and "Do not go gentle into that good night", a poem written in 1951 about his dying father.

Thoreau, Henry David

Henry David Thoreau (July 12, 1817 – May 6, 1862: born **David Henry Thoreau**) was an American author, naturalist, transcendentalist, tax resister, development critic, and philosopher who is best known for *Walden*, a reflection upon simple living in natural surroundings, and his essay, *Civil Disobedience*, an argument for individual resistance to civil government in moral opposition to an unjust state.

Thoreau's books, articles, essays, journals, and poetry total over 20 volumes. Among his lasting contributions were his writings on natural history and philosophy, where he anticipated the methods and findings of ecology and environmental history, two sources of modern day environmentalism.

Thurber, James

James Grover Thurber (December 8, 1894 – November 2, 1961) was a U.S. humorist and cartoonist. Thurber was best known for his contribution (both cartoons and short stories) to *The New Yorker* magazine.

Tolstoy, Leo

Count Lev Nikolayevich Tolstoy (September 9, 1828 – November 20, 1910) was a Russian writer – novelist, essayist, dramatist and philosopher as well as pacifist Christian anarchist and educational reformer. He was the most influential member of the aristocratic Tolstoy family.

As a fiction writer, Tolstoy is widely regarded as one of the greatest of all novelists, particularly noted for his masterpieces *War and Peace* and *Anna Karenina*. In their scope, breadth and realistic depiction of 19th-century Russian life, the two books stand at the peak of realist fiction. As a moral philosopher Tolstoy was notable for his ideas on nonviolent resistance through works such as *The Kingdom of God is Within You*, which in turn influenced such twentieth-century figures as Mohandas K. Gandhi and Martin Luther King, Jr.

Tomlin, Lily

Lily Tomlin (born September 1, 1939) is an Academy Award-nominated American actress, comedian, writer and producer. Tomlin's body of work, which has spanned over 40 years, has garnered her several Tony Awards and Emmy Awards, as well as a Grammy Award.

Tomlin was born **Mary Jean Tomlin** in Detroit, Michigan, daughter of Lillie Mae (née Ford), a housewife and nurse's aide who moved to Detroit from Paducah, Kentucky during the Great Depression, and Guy Tomlin, a factory worker. She is a 1957 graduate of Cass Technical High School. Tomlin attended Wayne State University, where her interest in the theater and performing arts began. After college, Tomlin began doing stand-up comedy in nightclubs in Detroit and later, in New York City. Her first television appearance was on *The Merv Griffin Show* in 1965.

In 1969, Tomlin joined the sketch comedy show *Laugh-In*. Her characters from the show have been associated with her throughout her career, including the gum-chewing, wisecracking, snorting telephone operator Ernestine, the bratty five-year old Edith Ann, rocking in her oversized chair, making rude noises, and telling stories about her baby brother and her dog, Buster, and the Tasteful Lady, who lives a gracious and naively entitled life in the upper class and shades of whom show up in Tomlin's film role in *All of Me*. Additional characters include Susie the Sorority Girl, who appeared on Tomlin's album *Modern Scream* and in her 1975 appearance on *Saturday Night Live*.

Truman, Harry S.

Harry S. Truman (May 8, 1884 – December 26, 1972) was the thirty-third President of the United States (1945 – 1953). As vice president, he succeeded to the office upon the death of Franklin D. Roosevelt.

During World War I he served as an artillery officer. After the war he became part of the political machine of Tom Pendergast and was elected a county judge in Missouri and eventually a United States Senator. In 1944, Roosevelt replaced Henry A. Wallace as vice president with Truman for Roosevelt's fourth term.

Tucker, Sophie

Sophie Tucker (January 13, 1884 – February 9, 1966) was a singer and comedian, one of the most popular entertainers in America during the first third of the 20th century.

She was born **Sonia Kalish** to a Jewish family in Tsarist Russia. Her family emigrated to the United States when she was an infant, and settled in Hartford, Connecticut. The family changed its name to Abuza, and her parents opened a restaurant.

Turner, Lana

Lana Turner (February 8, 1921 – June 29, 1995) was an Academy Award-nominated American film actress. On-screen, she was well-known for the glamour and sensuality she brought to almost all her movie roles. Off-screen, she led a stormy and colorful private life which included seven husbands, numerous lovers, and a famous murder scandal.

Twain, Mark

Samuel Langhorne Clemens (November 30, 1835 – April 21, 1910), better known by the pen name **Mark Twain**, was an American humanist, humorist, satirist, lecturer and writer. Twain is most noted for his novels *Adventures of Huckleberry Finn*,

which has since been called the Great American Novel, and *The Adventures of Tom Sawyer*. He is also known for his quotations. During his lifetime, Twain became a friend to presidents, artists, leading industrialists and European royalty.

Twain enjoyed immense public popularity, and his keen wit and incisive satire earned him praise from both critics and peers. American author William Faulkner called Twain "the father of American literature".

Vidal, Gore

Eugene Luther Gore Vidal (October 3, 1925 – July 31, 2012) was an American author of novels, stage plays, screenplays, and essays, and the scion of a prominent political family. He was an outspoken critic of the American political Establishment, and a noted wit and social critic who wrote the ground-breaking *The City and the Pillar* (1948) that outraged mainstream critics as the first major American novel to feature unambiguous homosexuality.

Villa, Pancho

Doroteo Arango Arámbula (June 5, 1878 – July 23, 1923), better known as **Francisco** or **"Pancho" Villa**, was a Mexican Revolutionary general. As commander of the *División del Norte* (Division of the North), he was the veritable caudillo of the Northern Mexican state of Chihuahua, which, due to its size, mineral wealth and proximity to the United States, made him a major player in Revolutionary military and politics. His charisma and effectiveness gave him great popularity, particularly in the North, and he was provisional Governor of Chihuahua in 1913 and 1914. While his violence and ambition prevented him from being accepted into the "pantheon" of national heroes until some twenty years after his death, today his memory is honored by many Mexicans. In addition, numerous streets and neighborhoods in Mexico are named in honor of him. In 1916 he raided Columbus, New Mexico. This act provoked the unsuccessful Punitive Expedition commanded by General John J. Pershing, which failed to capture Villa after a year in pursuit.

Voltaire

François-Marie Arouet (21 November 1694 – 30 May 1778), better known by the pen name **Voltaire**, was a French Enlightenment writer, essayist, deist and philosopher known for his wit, philosophical sport, and defense of civil liberties, including freedom of religion and the right to a fair trial. He was an outspoken supporter of social reform despite strict censorship laws and harsh penalties for those who broke them.

A satirical polemicist, he frequently made use of his works to criticize Christian Church dogma and the French institutions of his day.

Many of Voltaire's works and ideas would influence important thinkers of both the American and French Revolutions, an honor that he would share with other political theorists such as John Locke and Thomas Hobbes.

Walpole, Horace, 4th Earl of Orford

Horace Walpole, 4th Earl of Orford (24 September 1717 – 2 March 1797), more commonly known as **Horace Walpole**, was politician, writer, architectural innovator and cousin of Lord Nelson. His *Letters* are highly readable, and give a vivid picture of the more intellectual part of the aristocracy of his period.

Walters, Barbara

Barbara Jill Walters (born September 25, 1929) is an American journalist, writer and media personality who has been a regular fixture on morning television shows (*Today* and *The View*), an evening news magazine (*20/20*), and on *The ABC Evening News* as the first female evening news anchor. Walters was first known as a popular TV morning news anchor for over 10 years on NBC's *Today*, where she worked with Hugh Downs and later hosts Frank McGee and Jim Hartz. Walters later spent 25 years as co-host of ABC's newsmagazine *20/20*. She was the first woman to co-anchor the network evening news, working with Harry Reasoner on *The ABC Evening News*.

Washington, George

George Washington (February 22, 1732 – December 14, 1799) was a central, critical figure in the founding of the United States, as well as the nation's first president (1789 – 1797), after leading the Continental Army to victory over the Kingdom of Great Britain in the American Revolutionary War (1775 – 1783).

Washington was seen as symbolizing the new nation and republicanism in practice. His devotion to civic virtue made him an exemplary figure among early American politicians. During Washington's funeral oration, Henry Lee said that of all Americans, he was "first in war, first in peace, and first in the hearts of his countrymen". While often underrated by scholars, still consistently Washington is ranked first or in the first three with Abraham Lincoln and Franklin D. Roosevelt, both of whom radically altered the Constitutional government envisioned by Washington and the Founders, as one of the top three U.S. Presidents.

Washington, Martha

Martha Dandridge Custis Washington (June 2, 1731 – May 22, 1802) was the wife of George Washington, the first president of the United States. Although the title was not coined until after her death, Martha Washington is considered to be the first First Lady of the United States. During her lifetime, she was simply known as "Lady Washington".

Watson, James D.

James Dewey Watson (born April 6, 1928) is an American molecular biologist, best known as one of the co-discoverers of the structure of DNA. Watson, Francis Crick, and Maurice Wilkins were awarded the 1962 Nobel Prize in Physiology or Medicine "for their discoveries concerning the molecular structure of nucleic acids and its significance for information transfer in living material".

Waugh, Evelyn

Arthur Evelyn St. John Waugh (October 28, 1903 – April 10, 1966) was an English writer, best known for such satirical novels as *Decline and Fall*, *Vile Bodies*, *Scoop*, *A Handful of Dust* and *The Loved One*, as well as for broader and more personal works, such as *Brideshead Revisited* and the *Sword of Honour* trilogy, that are influenced by his own experiences and his conservative and Catholic viewpoints. Many of Waugh's novels depict British aristocracy and high society, which he satirizes but to which, paradoxically, he was also strongly attracted. In addition, he wrote short stories, three biographies, and the first volume of an unfinished autobiography. His travel writings and his extensive diaries and correspondence have also been published.

Wells, Carolyn

Carolyn Wells (June 18, 1862 – March 26, 1942) was an American author and poet. After finishing school she worked as a librarian for the Rahway Library Association. Her first book, *At the Sign of the Sphinx* (1896), was a collection of charades. Her next publications were *The Jingle Book* and *The Story of Betty* (1899), followed by a book of verse entitled *Idle Idyls* (1900). After 1900, Wells wrote numerous novels and collections of poetry. Carolyn Wells wrote a total of more than 170 books.

Wells, H. G.

Herbert George Wells (September 21, 1866 – August 13, 1946), better known as **H. G. Wells**, was an English writer best known for such science fiction novels as *The Time Machine*, *The War of the Worlds*, *The Invisible Man*, *The First Men in the Moon* and *The Island of Doctor Moreau*. He was a prolific writer of both fiction and non-fiction, and produced works in many different genres, including contemporary novels, history, and social commentary. He was also an outspoken socialist. His later works become increasingly political and didactic, and only his early science fiction novels are widely read today. Wells and Jules Verne are each sometimes referred to as "The Father of Science Fiction."

West, Mae

Mae West (August 17, 1893 – November 22, 1980) was an American actress, playwright, screenwriter, and sex symbol.

Famous for her bawdy double entendres, West made a name for herself in vaudeville and on the stage in New York before moving to Hollywood to become a comedian, actress and writer in the motion picture industry.

One of the most controversial stars of her day, West encountered many problems including censorship.

When her cinematic career ended, she continued to perform on stage, in Las Vegas, in the United Kingdom, on radio and television, and recorded rock and roll albums.

Wharton, Edith

Edith Wharton (January 24, 1862 – August 11, 1937) was an American novelist, short story writer, and designer.

Wharton was born **Edith Newbold Jones** to the wealthy New York family often associated with the phrase "Keeping up with the Joneses". She combined her insider's view of America's privileged classes with a brilliant, natural wit to write humorous and incisive novels and short stories. As such, she was well-acquainted with many of her era's literary and public figures, including Henry James and Theodore Roosevelt.

Wilde, Oscar

Oscar Fingal O'Flahertie Wills Wilde (October 16, 1854 – November 30, 1900) was an Irish playwright, novelist, poet, and author of short stories. Known for his barbed wit, he was one of the most successful playwrights of late Victorian London, and one of the greatest celebrities of his day. As the result of a famous trial, he suffered a dramatic downfall and was imprisoned for two years of hard labour after being convicted of the offence of "gross indecency".

Will, George

George Frederick Will (born May 4, 1941) is a Pulitzer Prize-winning, conservative American newspaper columnist, journalist, and author.

Williams, Robin

Robin McLaurin Williams (July 21, 1951 – August 11, 2014) is an Academy Award-winning American actor and comedian who has done television, stage, and film work.

Wilson, Tom (cartoonist)

Tom Wilson (born August 1, 1931) is an American cartoonist. Born in Grant Town, Marion County, West Virginia, he is the creator of the comic strip Ziggy, and drew it from 1971 to 1987. After that it was continued by his son, Tom Wilson II.

Wilson, Woodrow

Thomas Woodrow Wilson (December 28, 1856 – February 3, 1924) was the twenty-eighth President of the United States. A devout Presbyterian and leading "intellectual" of the Progressive Era, he served as president of Princeton University then became the reform governor of New Jersey in 1910. With Theodore Roosevelt and William Howard Taft dividing the Republican vote, Wilson was elected President as a Democrat in 1912. He proved highly successful in leading a Democratic Congress to pass major legislation including the Federal Trade Commission, the Clayton Antitrust Act, the Underwood Tariff, the Federal Farm Loan Act and most notably the Federal Reserve System.

Narrowly re-elected in 1916, his second term centered on World War I. He tried to maintain U.S. neutrality, but when Germany began unrestricted submarine warfare he wrote several admonishing notes to Germany. Subsequently he asked Congress to declare war on the Central Powers. He focused on diplomacy and financial considerations, leaving the waging of the war primarily in the hands of the military establishment.

On the home front he began the first effected draft in 1917, raised billions through Liberty loans, imposed an income tax, set up the War Industries Board, promoted labor union growth, supervised agriculture and food production through the Lever Act, took over control of the railroads, and suppressed anti-war movements. He paid surprisingly little attention to military affairs, but provided the funding and food supplies that helped the Americans in the war and hastened Allied victory in 1918.

Winchell, Walter

Walter Winchell (April 7, 1897 – February 20, 1972), an American newspaper and radio commentator, invented the gossip column at the *New York Evening Graphic*. He broke the journalistic taboo against exposing the private lives of public figures, permanently altering the shape of journalism and celebrity. He was a top gossip reporter, whose newspaper column and radio show could make or break a celebrity.

Windsor, Duke of

The peerage title **Duke of Windsor** was created in the Peerage of the United Kingdom in 1937 for "The Prince Edward, formerly King of the United Kingdom," as well as each of the other Commonwealth realms. Edward (June 23, 1894 – May 28, 1972) had abdicated on 11 December 1936 so that he could marry the American divorcee Wallis Simpson, who became the **Duchess of Windsor**. At the time of the abdication there was much controversy as to what the ex-King should be referred to – other possibilities were the Dukedoms of Cambridge or Connaught (although neither was likely because the Marquessate of Cambridge and the Dukedom of Connaught were both extant at the time). One theory is that it was Prime Minister Stanley Baldwin's idea to give him the title Duke of Windsor. Another is that it was the new King George VI who brought up the idea of a title just after the abdication instrument was signed, and suggested using "the family name" (recounted in the Duke's memoir *A King's Story*).

Winfrey, Oprah

Oprah Gail Winfrey (born January 29, 1954) is the American multiple-Emmy Award winning host of *The Oprah Winfrey Show*, which was for many years the highest-rated talk show in television history. She is also an influential book critic, an Academy Award-nominated actress, and a magazine publisher. She has been ranked the richest African American of the 20th century, the most philanthropic African American of all time, and the world's only black billionaire for three straight years. She is also according to some assessments, the most influential woman in the world.

Winters, Jonathan

Jonathan Harshman Winters III (November 11, 1925 – April 11, 2013) was an American comedian and actor.

After attending private boarding school at Culver Military Academy in Culver, Indiana, Winters enlisted in the Marines at age 17 and served in the South Pacific during World War II. After his discharge he studied cartooning at Dayton Art Institute, where he met Eileen Schauder, whom he married in 1948. He began comedy routines and acting while studying at Kenyon College in Gambier, Ohio. He was also a local radio personality at WIZE in Springfield, Ohio.

Beginning as a stand-up comic with a madcap wildness, Winters recorded many classic comedy albums. Probably the best known of his characters from this period is Maudie Frickert, the seemingly sweet old lady with the barbed tongue. He was a favorite of Jack Paar and appeared frequently on his television programs. In addition, he would often appear on the *Tonight Show* with Johnny Carson, usually in the guise of some character. Carson often did not know what Winters had planned and usually had to tease out the character's back story through the course of the interview.

Winters, Shelley

Shelley Winters (August 18, 1920 – January 14, 2006) was an American actress who won Academy Awards for her supporting roles in *The Diary of Anne Frank* and *A Patch of Blue*, and a

Golden Globe Award for her role in *The Poseidon Adventure*. She appeared in dozens of films as well as on stage and television.

Wodehouse, P. G.

Sir Pelham Grenville Wodehouse, KBE (15 October 1881 – 14 February 1975) was a comic writer who had enjoyed enormous popular success for more than seventy years. Despite all the political and social upheavals that occurred during his life, much of which was spent in France and the United States, Wodehouse's main canvas remained that of prewar English upper-class society, reflecting his birth, education, and youthful writing career.

An acknowledged master of English prose, Wodehouse was admired both by contemporaries like Hilaire Belloc, Evelyn Waugh and Rudyard Kipling as well as by modern writers like Douglas Adams, Salman Rushdie and Terry Pratchett. Sean O'Casey famously called him "English literature's performing flea", a description that Wodehouse used as the title of a collection of his letters to a friend, Bill Townend.

Best known today for the Jeeves and Blandings Castle novels and short stories, Wodehouse was also a talented playwright and lyricist who was part author and writer of fifteen plays and 250 lyrics for some thirty musical comedies. He worked with Cole Porter on the musical *Anything Goes* (1934) and frequently collaborated with Jerome Kern and Guy Bolton. He wrote the lyrics for the hit song "Bill" in Kern's *Show Boat* (1927), wrote the lyrics for the Gershwin – Romberg musical *Rosalie* (1928), and collaborated with Rudolph Friml on a musical version of *The Three Musketeers* (1928).

Wolfe, Tom

Thomas Kennerly Wolfe (born March 2, 1931 in Richmond, Virginia), known as **Tom Wolfe**, is a best-selling American author and journalist. He is one of the founders of the New Journalism movement of the 1960s and 1970s.

Wordsworth, William

William Wordsworth (April 7, 1770 – April 23, 1850) was a major English romantic poet who, with Samuel Taylor Coleridge, helped launch the Romantic Age in English literature with their 1798 joint publication, *Lyrical Ballads*.

Wordsworth's masterpiece is generally considered to be *The Prelude*, an autobiographical poem of his early years which the poet revised and expanded a number of times. The work was posthumously titled and published, prior to which it was generally known as the poem "to Coleridge". Wordsworth was England's Poet Laureate from 1843 until his death in 1850.

Wouk, Herman

Herman Wouk (born May 27, 1915) is a best selling American author with a number of notable novels to his credit, including *The Caine Mutiny*, *The Winds of War*, and *War and Remembrance*.

Wright, Frank Lloyd

Frank Lloyd Wright (June 8, 1867 – April 9, 1959) was one of the world's most prominent and influential architects.

He developed a series of highly individual styles, influenced the design of buildings all over the world, and to this day remains America's most famous architect.

Wright was also well known in his lifetime. His colorful personal life frequently made headlines, most notably for the failure of his first two marriages and for the 1914 fire and murders at his Taliesin studio.

Youngman, Henny

Henry "Henny" Youngman (March 16, 1906 – February 24, 1998) was a British-born American comedian and violinist famous for "one-liners", short, simple jokes usually delivered rapid-fire. His best known (and often misattributed) one-liner was "Take my wife – please".

Index of Quotations by Author

Adams, Henry Brooks
Page: 219

Ade, George
Page: 70

Adenauer, Konrad
Page: 18

Ali, Muhammad
Pages; 82, 83

Allen, Fred
Pages; 31, 61

Allen, Woody
Pages; 6, 67, 70, 71, 103, 108, 109, 112, 113, 115, 124, 179, 180, 251, 254, 255

Amis, Kingsley
Page: 179

Amory, Cleveland
Page: 182

Aquinas, Thomas
Page: 119

Aristotle
Pages; 32, 45, 65, 70, 73, 74, 201, 210, 223, 229, 233, 266

Augustine of Hippo
Page: 106, 210

Aurelius, Marcus
Page: 277

Bacall, Lauren
Page: 63

Bacon, Francis
Page: 266

Baez, Joan
Page: 75

Balfour, Arthur
Page: 209

Ball, Lucille
Page: 270

Balzac, Honoré de
Page: 272

Bankhead, Tallulah
Pages; 58, 278

Barber, Jerry
Page: 77

Barkley, Alben W.
Page: 92

Barnum, P. T.
Pages; 2, 24, 29

Barry, Dave
    Page: 31
Barrymore, John
    Pages; 111, 124, 130, 136, 137, 144, 288
Beaumarchais, Pierre
    Page: 222
Behan, Brendan
    Pages; 94, 107
Bellow, Saul
    Page: 154
Bentham, Jeremy
    Page: 43
Berenson, Bernard
    Page: 22
Berra, Yogi
    Pages; 8, 78, 80
Bhartrihari
    Pages; 121, 147
Bierce, Ambrose
    Pages: 48, 95, 120, 147, 195, 260
Billings, Josh
    Pages; 146, 206
Bismarck, Otto von
    Pages; 232, 233
Blair, Tony
    Page: 222
Blake, Eubie
    Page: 268
Blake, William
    Page: 191
Blount, Jr., Roy
    Page: 42
Bonaparte, Napoleon
    Pages; 93, 163, 191, 208, 221, 243, 257, 280
Bombeck, Erma
    Pages; 33, 180

Boorstin, Daniel J.
    Page: 61
Brando, Marlon
    Page: 60
Brezhnev, Leonid
    Page: 229
Bright, John
    Page: 168
Brooks, Mel
    Page: 216
Brown, Helen Gurley
    Page: 149
Buckley, Jr., William F.
    Pages; 32, 234
Burns, George
    Pages; 57, 103, 274
Burroughs, John
    Page: 243
Burton, Richard
    Page: 95
Butler, Samuel
    Page: 131
Caesar, Julius
    Page: 197
Camden, William
    Page: 44
Canterbury, Tommy
    Page: 85
Cantor, Eddie
    Page: 37
Capp, Al
    Page: 55
Capote, Truman
    Page: 109
Carlyle, Thomas
    Page: 48

Index of Quotations by Author

Carson, Johnny
Pages; 63, 253
Carter, Lillian Gordy
Page: 182
Catullus
Page: 122
Chamfort, Nicolas
Page: 112
Chanel, Coco
Page: 119
Chekhov, Anton
Page: 59
Cher
Page: 134
Cherry, Don
Page: 84
Chesterfield, Earl of
Pages; 25, 111
Chesterton, G. K.
Pages; 17, 46, 56, 137, 157
Child, Julia
Page: 278
Churchill, Winston
Pages; 9, 93, 209, 222, 255, 256, 257
Ciardi, John
Page: 7
Cicero
Pages; 2, 25, 93, 158, 190, 197, 232, 271
Clancy, Tom
Page: 110
Colette
Page: 176
Confucius
Page: 36
Cosby, Bill
Pages; 36, 179

Coward, Noel
Page: 27
Crawford, Joan
Page: 120
Crisp, Quentin
Page: 264
Dalí, Salvador
Page: 286
Dangerfield, Rodney
Pages; 84, 135
Darrow, Clarence
Page: 181
De Gaulle, Charles
Pages; 217, 220
De Kooning, Willem
Page: 7
Dean, Dizzy
Page: 81
Demaret, Jimmy
Page: 78
Dewar, Tommy
Page: 21
Dietrich, Marlene
Page: 125
Diller, Phyllis
Pages; 115, 123
Diogenes of Sinope
Page: 108
Dirksen, Everett
Page: 8
Disraeli, Benjamin
Pages; 196, 218, 287
Dostoevsky, Fyodor
Page: 157
Douglas, Kirk
Page: 180

Dunne, Finley Peter
  Page: 68
Eban, Abba
  Page: 166
Edison, Thomas
  Pages; 19, 24, 37
Einstein, Albert
  Pages; 162, 220
Eisenhower, Dwight D.
  Page: 220
Eliot, T. S.
  Page: 45
Emerson, Ralph Waldo
  Pages; 6, 53, 96, 159, 164, 171, 188, 202, 266, 282
Fields, W. C.
  Pages; 4, 28, 33, 87, 89, 91, 94, 96, 147, 152, 175, 253, 261, 283
Fischler, Stan
  Page: 84
Flaubert, Gustave
  Pages; 226, 280
Florus
  Page: 143
Flynn, Errol
  Page: 11
Forbes, Malcolm
  Pages; 3, 27
Ford, Henry
  Page: 74
Foreman, George
  Page: 82
France, Anatole
  Pages; 127, 239, 242
Franklin, Benjamin
  Pages; 1, 2, 17, 25, 29, 41, 69, 94, 98, 140, 144, 188, 193, 221, 234, 237

Freud, Sigmund
  Pages; 118, 240
Friedman, Milton
  Pages; 28, 231, 233
Frost, Robert
  Pages; 27, 33, 34, 35, 44, 72, 123, 137, 269
Gabor, Eva
  Page: 126
Gabor, Zsa Zsa
  Pages; 114, 129
Galbraith, John Kenneth
  Pages; 31, 219
Galsworthy, John
  Page: 32
Gauguin, Paul
  Page: 288
George, David Lloyd
  Pages; 213, 232
Gleason, Jackie
  Page: 60
Goethe, Johann Wolfgang von
  Page: 40
Goldwyn, Samuel
  Pages; 62, 63, 254
Gourmont, Remy de
  Page: 105
Grant, Cary
  Page: 270
Graves, Robert
  Page: 45
Greeley, Horace
  Page: 100
Gretzky, Wayne
  Page: 85
Guinness, Alec
  Page: 60

Hamilton, Alexander
Page: 159

Heine, Heinrich
Pages; 119, 148

Heinlein, Robert A.
Page: 239

Hemingway, Ernest
Pages; 99, 120, 261

Hepburn, Katharine
Page: 59

Herford, Oliver
Page: 60

Herold, Don
Page: 151

Hitchcock, Alfred
Page: 261

Hitler, Adolf
Pages; 207, 228

Holmes, Jr., Oliver Wendell
Pages; 19, 44, 86

Hoover, Herbert
Page: 263

Hope, Bob
Page: 274

Hopper, Edward
Page: 52

Horne, Lena
Page: 30

Hubbard, Kin
Pages; 11, 30, 146, 191, 199, 218, 248

Hughes, Rupert
Page: 148

Hugo, Victor
Page: 22

Hume, David
Page: 284

Huxley, Aldous
Pages; 23, 168, 206, 258

Huxley, Thomas Henry
Page: 197

Ingersoll, Robert G.
Page: 245

Jackson, Stonewall
Page: 97

James, William
Page: 21

Jefferson, Thomas
Page: 285

Jesus
Page: 244

Johnson, Lyndon B.
Pages; 8, 40, 70, 134, 199

Johnson, Samuel
Pages; 50, 100

Joubert, Joseph
Page: 16

Joyce, James
Page: 108

Kant, Immanuel
Page: 172

Kaufman, George S.
Page: 58

Keillor, Garrison
Pages; 104, 252

Kennedy, Florynce
Page: 105

Kennedy, John F.
Pages; 20, 218

Kennedy, Rose Fitzgerald
Page: 287

Keynes, John Maynard
Page: 68

Khayyám, Omar
Page: 98

Khrushchev, Nikita
Page: 214

Kierkegaard, Soren
Pages; 231, 279

King, Frank
Page: 87

King, Jr., Martin Luther
Page: 21

Kipling, Rudyard
Page: 272

Kissinger, Henry
Pages; 20, 111, 196, 214

Kraus, Karl
Pages; 217, 277

Lauder, Estée
Page: 125

Lebowitz, Fran
Pages; 174, 176

Lee, Gypsy Rose
Page: 104

Leno, Jay
Page: 146

Levant, Oscar
Page: 284

Levenson, Sam
Page: 172

Lincoln, Abraham
Pages; 24, 34, 138, 186, 200, 202, 248

Locke, John
Page: 230

Long, Huey
Page: 34

Longfellow, Henry Wadsworth
Pages; 99, 185

Loren, Sophia
Page: 282

Louis, Joe
Page: 11

Lowell, James Russell
Page: 226

Luther, Martin
Page: 149

Macaulay, Thomas Babington
Page: 23

Macauley, Ed
Page: 87

Machiavelli, Niccolò
Pages; 192, 223

MacIver, Robert Morrison
Page: 72

Magrane, Joe
Page: 81

Mailer, Norman
Pages; 140, 216

Mantle, Mickey
Page: 78

Marquis, Don
Pages; 22, 193, 201

Martial
Pages; 190, 258

Martin, Dean
Page: 95

Marx, Groucho
Pages; 67, 107, 129, 135, 136, 139, 150, 151, 152, 154, 219, 267

Maugham, W. Somerset
Pages; 132, 264

Meir, Golda
Page: 273

Menander
Pages; 66, 144

Index of Quotations by Author

Mencken, H. L.
Pages; 10, 24, 46, 47, 61, 79, 97, 113, 118, 129, 132, 140, 143, 145, 158, 161, 165, 187, 193, 194, 205, 213, 214, 215, 220, 225, 227, 228, 238, 240, 241, 242, 246, 247, 252, 259, 268, 269, 279, 282, 288

Montesquieu, Charles de Secondat, baron de
Page: 230

Moore, Roger
Page: 4

Mull, Martin
Page: 174

Munro, Hector Hugh
Pages; 39, 173, 204

Namath, Joe
Page: 79

Nash, Ogden
Page: 90

Nathan, George Jean
Pages; 15, 92

Nepos, Cornelius
Page: 189

Nettles, Graig
Page: 80

Niebuhr, Reinhold
Page: 227

Nietzsche, Friedrich
Pages; 15, 49, 50, 73, 119, 138, 165, 166, 200, 208, 237, 241, 244, 259, 260

Nixon, Richard
Page: 221

Onassis, Aristotle
Pages; 6, 153

Orben, Robert
Page: 182

O'Rourke, P. J.
Page: 213

Orwell, George
Page: 265

Ovid
Page: 145

Paine, Thomas
Pages; 23, 231, 247

Park, Brad
Page: 85

Parker, Dorothy
Pages; 3, 48, 61, 62, 89, 91, 114, 150, 154, 177, 261

Parton, Dolly
Page: 62

Peale, Norman Vincent
Page: 189

Peter, Laurence J.
Pages; 66, 79, 226

Phaedrus
Page: 18

Picasso, Pablo
Pages; 5, 54, 126

Plato
Pages; 16, 73, 118, 157, 159, 171, 207, 215

Plautus
Pages; 1, 121, 122, 145, 148

Pliny the Younger
Pages; 165, 223

Poe, Edgar Allan
Page: 178

Pope, Alexander
Pages; 65, 162, 163, 286

Pope John XXIII
Page: 265

Presley, Elvis
  Page: 49
Priestley, J. B.
  Page: 181
Pryor, Richard
  Page: 130
Puzo, Mario
  Pages; 43, 47
Quintilian, Marcus Fabius
  Page: 235
Rawlings, Marjorie Kinnan
  Page: 117
Renoir, Pierre-Auguste
  Page: 272
Repplier, Agnes
  Page: 118
Reston, James
  Page: 234
Robinson, Sugar Ray
  Page: 83
Rochefoucauld, François de La
  Page: 195
Rockefeller, John D.
  Page: 4
Rockefeller, Nelson
  Page: 127
Rodriguez, Juan "Chi-Chi"
  Page: 77
Rogers, Ginger
  Page: 122
Rogers, Will
  Pages; 12, 39, 69, 163, 187, 196, 216, 229
Roosevelt, Franklin D.
  Page: 19
Rostand, Jean
  Page: 242

Rousseau, Jean-Jacques
  Page: 185
Runyon, Damon
  Page: 87
Russell, Bertrand
  Pages; 35, 69, 237, 240, 245, 279
Safire, William
  Page: 68
Saget, Bob
  Page: 174
Santayana, George
  Pages; 16, 280
Sargent, John Singer
  Page: 54
Schulz, Charles M.
  Page: 161
Scott-Maxwell, Florida
  Page: 177
Seneca the Elder
  Pages; 188, 238
Shakespeare, William
  Pages; 17, 104, 112, 194, 204
Shaw, George Bernard
  Pages; 5, 10, 40, 41, 57, 72, 75, 86, 99, 100, 106, 115, 121, 123, 134, 152, 190, 194, 200, 209, 215, 225, 263, 277, 278, 286
Sheridan, Richard Brinsley
  Page: 205
Smith, Sydney
  Page: 186
Socrates
  Pages; 21, 131, 171, 281
Sowell, Thomas
  Page: 199
Spinks, Leon
  Page: 82

Squire, J. C.
Page: 90

Stalin, Joseph
Pages; 208, 232, 257

Stengel, Casey
Pages; 81, 106

Stevenson, Adlai
Page: 217

Stevenson, Robert Louis
Page: 138

Stewart, James (actor)
Page: 270

Strachey, Lytton
Page: 251

Sutton, Don
Page: 80

Swift, Jonathan
Pages; 42, 246, 265

Syrus, Publilius
Pages; 10, 16, 23, 30, 113, 117, 123, 125, 126, 185, 192

Tacitus
Page: 192

Talleyrand-Périgord, Charles Maurice de
Page: 149

Teresa, Mother
Page: 117

Thomas, Dylan
Page: 91

Thoreau, Henry David
Pages; 160, 164, 187, 230, 261

Thurber, James
Page: 216

Tolstoy, Leo
Page: 186

Tomlin, Lily
Pages; 35, 209

Truman, Harry S.
Pages; 55, 206

Tucker, Sophie
Pages; 3, 271

Turner, Lana
Page: 133

Twain, Mark
Pages; 1, 7, 20, 29, 33, 41, 42, 43, 47, 49, 56, 66, 67, 69, 71, 75, 86, 92, 97, 98, 110, 139, 151, 158, 160, 161, 162, 164, 167, 173, 175, 176, 181, 189, 201, 203, 204, 205, 207, 235, 245, 251, 252, 253, 254, 256, 260, 261, 264, 267, 273, 281, 283, 287

Vidal, Gore
Pages; 173, 178, 255

Villa, Pancho
Page: 256

Voltaire
Pages; 9, 18, 50, 105, 139, 227, 228, 230, 243, 244, 247, 248

Walpole, Horace, 4th Earl of Orford
Page: 166

Walters, Barbara
Page: 172

Washington, George
Page: 193

Washington, Martha
Page: 285

Watson, James D.
Page: 74

Waugh, Evelyn
Page: 177

Wells, Carolyn
Page: 203

Wells, H. G.
Page: 246

West, Mae
  Pages; 107, 114, 133, 136, 150, 153
Wharton, Edith
  Page: 285
Wilde, Oscar
  Pages; 9, 28, 46, 53, 54, 58, 59, 109, 124, 127, 130, 131, 135, 143, 153, 167, 178, 202, 258, 260, 263, 267, 268, 269, 271, 273, 274, 283
Will, George
  Page: 235
Williams, Robin
  Page: 4
Wilson, Tom
  Page: 203
Wilson, Woodrow
  Page: 15
Winchell, Walter
  Page: 62

Windsor, Duke of
  Page: 175
Winfrey, Oprah
  Page: 36
Winters, Jonathan
  Page: 37
Winters, Shelley
  Page: 133
Wodehouse, P. G.
  Page: 86
Wolfe, Tom
  Page: 238
Wordsworth, William
  Page: 90
Wouk, Herman
  Page: 12
Wright, Frank Lloyd
  Pages; 39, 281
Youngman, Henny
  Page: 110

BUY THIS BOOK

SNAPPY SAYINGS is available at
AMAZOM.COM and BARNES&NOBLE.COM
or you can order it at any bookstore in America
for delivery within a few days.

ABOUT THE AUTHOR

BRADFORD G. WHELER is the former CEO, President and Co-owner of Allan Electric Company. He sold Allan Electric to a New York Stock Exchange listed company. After staying on as President during the transition, Brad retired.

Brad's lifelong love of history, art, books, and the inherent humor in man's nature led to the founding of BookCollaborative.com and the publishing of Inca's Death Cave as well as *GOLF SAYINGS: wit & wisdom of a good walk spoiled, CAT SAYINGS: wit & wisdom from the whiskered ones, HORSE SAYINGS: wit & wisdom straight from the horse's mouth, DOG SAYINGS: wit & wisdom from man's best friend,* and *Inca's Death Cave: An Archaeological Adventure Novel.*

His community involvements include being a Trustee of Community General Hospital in Hamilton, NY, and chairing their Finance Committee. He is the former Chairman of the Board of Trustees of Cazenovia College, and former Chairman and member of the Board of Directors and Alumni Association and President of the Sigma Phi Society at Cornell University in Ithaca, NY. He is also a former member of the Board of Directors of the Greater Cazenovia Area Chamber of Commerce and several other boards.

Brad played polo on the Cornell University men's polo team for four years and was a member of the Cazenovia Polo Club. In 2012 he was inducted into the Manlius Pebble Hill Athletic Hall of Fame.
He holds a BS and ME in Civil and Environmental Engineering from Cornell University in Ithaca, NY as well as an MBA degree from Fordham University in New York, NY.

Brad, his wife, Julie, and their golden retriever Quincy live in Cazenovia, NY and Fort Pierce, FL.

Buy These Books at a discount on www.BookCollaborative.com

They are also available on Amazon.com and Barnes&Noble.com. You can order them at any bookstore in the US, UK, and Canada for delivery within in a few days.

GOLF SAYINGS
wit & wisdom of a good walk spoiled

Five 5 Star reviews

Lots and lots of wisdom on these pages and a lot of chuckles

By D. Blankenship, Amazon top 50 and Hall of Fame reviewer.

I have quite a few books whose subject matter deals exclusively with "golf sayings." I have been collecting these books since I first started playing some 55 odd years ago. Of all the wonderful reading I have on my shelf; all the wisdom, humor and frustration documented in their pages concerning what is probably the greatest game every invented, this little work is most certainly in the exclusive top five I own.

CAT SAYINGS
wit & wisdom from the whiskered ones

Thirteen 5 Star and three 4 Star reviews

Feline Art and Words: For cat lovers and those who attempt to understand them

By Grady Harp, Amazon top 50 and Hall of Fame Reviewer

Brad G. Wheler has curated an art and words spectrum devoted to Cats (note the capital C and you'll get the gist of this book!). There is about as much variety of artwork reproduced on every page of this enormously entertaining book as is mirrored in the variety of excerpts of words from the ancients to the moderns. Wheler wisely keeps the reader's interest by dividing his book into chapters: Cats Rule, Wild Cats, Kittens, Humor, Of Cats and Dogs, The Cat Personality, Death of a Friend, Love Of, Cats Vs. People - each topic is generously illustrated with art and comments pertinent to each subsection.

HORSE SAYINGS
wit & wisdom straight from the horse's mouth

Nine 5 Star and two 4 Star reviews

Horse Enthusiasts Rejoice!

By Dr. Joseph S. Maresca, Amazon top 1000 and Hall of Fame reviewer

Horse Sayings; Wit and Wisdom Straight from the Horse's Mouth by Bradford G. Wheler depicts the horse in all of its glory together with the continued human interest in the equine. The presentation has pearls of wisdom from horse humor, competition, ancient wisdom, training and many other aspects of horses unbeknownst to the public generally but well known to horse enthusiasts. There are illustrations by 61 artists from 11 countries.

DOG SAYINGS
wit & wisdom from man's best friend

Three 5 Star reviews

A Choice Read, Solidly Recommended

By Midwest Book Review

The simple mutts can be far wiser than they let on. *Dog Sayings; Wit & Wisdom from Man's Best Friend* looks at a collection of humor and knowledge as well as plenty of art focusing on man's constant canine companion. For centuries, there has been much said about the relationship of man and dog, and much inspiration has been drawn from them. Presented in full color throughout, *Dog Sayings* is a choice read, solidly recommended.

```
SNAPPY SAYINGS
wit & wisdom from
the world's greatest minds
```

Four 5 Star reviews

A Top Pick for Anyone Looking for
a Solid Collection of Humor

By Midwest Book Review

The best wit and wisdom comes from the best minds. Snappy Sayings is a compilation of quips from countless brilliant minds throughout history, from hundreds of years ago to the modern day. Divided into the many aspects of human nature and the unique quips delivered from these individuals, *Snappy Sayings* is a collection that will lead to hours of entertainment. *Snappy Sayings* is a top pick for anyone looking for a solid collection of humor.

```
EIGHTEEN 6/10/71
```

`The Poetry Of John G. Hunter III` is a collection of poems written by John G. Hunter III and given to Bradford G. Wheler for his eighteenth birthday on June 10th 1971. Each poem is accompanied by a color photograph. The layout and design was done by the renowned Italian book designer Adira Cucicov. Wheler has said many times, "I'm sure I received many fine gifts on my 18th birthday but this is the only one I remember and still treasure."

www.ingramcontent.com/pod-product-compliance
Lightning Source LLC
Chambersburg PA
CBHW080453110426
42742CB00017B/2878